# Post-Abortion Aftermath: A Comprehensive Consideration

Writings generated by various experts at a "Post-Abortion Summit Conference"

*Edited by*
*Michael T. Mannion*

**Sheed & Ward**

Sheed & Ward™ is a service of The National Catholic Reporter Publishing Company.

◆

**Library of Congress Cataloguing-in-Publication Data**

Post-abortion aftermath : a comprehensive consideration / edited by
   Michael T. Mannion.
          p.     cm.
      Papers originally presented at the Post-Abortion Aftermath
   Conference, Washington Retreat House, Washington, D.C., held
   in Sept. 1993.
      Includes bibliographical references.
      ISBN: 1-55612-708-1
      1. Abortion—United States—Psychological aspects—Congresses.
   2. Abortion—United States—Religious aspects—Congresses.
   3. Abortion—United States—Moral and ethical aspects—Congresses.
   4. Abortion counseling—United States—Congresses.  I. Mannion,
   Michael T.
   HQ767.5.U5P67   1994
   155.9'3—dc20                                        94-21556
                                                           CIP

◆

Published by:  Sheed & Ward
               115 E. Armour Blvd.
               P.O. Box 419492
               Kansas City, MO 64141

To order, call: (800) 333-7373
*Cover design by John Murello.*

# Contents

# 1

## Opening Remarks

### *Cardinal James A. Hickey*

"We are one body, one body in Christ. . . . And we do not stand
alone. . . . And He came that we might have life."

These are the words that tens of thousands of our young people and our Holy Father, John Paul II, sang out in Denver just a few
short weeks ago.

These are the words that I now choose to welcome you, my
brother bishops, visiting priests, and our eminent presenters and
guests. I thank you for coming to this very important conference,
which I believe may be the first of its kind in its scope and participation.

Truly, we have not come alone. We have come with a very
important and common concern: to help heal the Body of Christ.

The second verse of the song continues:

"Can you hear them crying, can you feel their pain?
Will you feed my hungry, will you help my lame?
See the unborn baby, the forgotten one,
They are not forsaken, they are not unloved."

The feeling in the words, the power of the song—sung by people from the Body of Christ spanning every corner of our planet—
brought many to tears.

Our presence here verifies that, truly, they are not forsaken,
unloved, or forgotten. And that we as members and leaders in the
Body of Christ wish to learn the lessons that their lives—and, unfortunately, their deaths—have taught us. We come as part of that
Body of Christ, seeking to be the Lord's instruments to help heal
those who are broken, to help those who stand on the precipice of
the decisions of death to avoid them.

In a very real sense, this conference is an enfleshment of what our Holy Father said and called for in Denver (to paraphrase): "Only the truth will set you free." Nothing else. No one else.

For these two brief days we seek to explore the truth of the sacredness of human life and the consequences for all those involved when that life is lost by abortion.

We wish to learn how together we can better articulate and then integrate this message into the Church's pastoral and sacramental life. You who have come have given many years of yours lives to the cause of healing. This conference, initiated by Cardinal Trujillo, is the Church's way of saying, "We need to hear what you have learned." The Body of Christ is never so alive and filled with the Spirit of Jesus as when it reaches out to its sons and daughters with love and compassion.

"We are one body. We do not stand alone." Thank you for coming.

PRAYER:

> "God Our Father—you sent your Son, Jesus, into our world that He might teach us not only who He is, but also who we are. We learn the message of the journey of faith that takes us from Bethlehem to Jerusalem—from birth to death—and then to Eternal Life. We pray today for all those whose lives have led us to commit ourselves to walk with them along their journey of faith as they seek healing within themselves, with others, and with you. We pray for ourselves, as well, that these special days that we share together may bear fruit in our Church—the Body of Christ—and that you might continue to bless us with the privilege of the ministry of post-abortion reconciliation and healing. Through it, you help us turn grief to grace. We ask you to hear us through Jesus Christ, your Son, Our Lord."
>
> AMEN.

# 2

## The Vision and Principles of the Post-Abortion Healing Process\*

---

I. UNIQUENESS AND DEPTH OF POST-ABORTION AFTERMATH

  A. Post-abortion aftermath is a unique collection of stress and grief-related symptoms stemming from deep and complicated conflicts set in motion by an abortion. These symptoms have been largely ignored and have tended to isolate and alienate those individuals who have experienced the tragedy of abortion.

  B. This aftermath includes but is not limited to the following:

    1. Complicated and unresolved grief—struggling to mourn the loss that one has experienced from contributing to the death of the child;

    2. Emotional conflicts—guilt, shame, and depression arising from the awareness of the consequences following the destruction of a unique human life that God has entrusted to a family;

    3. Identity crisis—stemming from the realization that one is capable of and has taken a human life;

    4. Disrupted relationships—rooted in an inability to deal with the loss of a child. Alienation, rejection, hostility, friction, tension are manifested in family relationships, with friends, and with God and the Church. This includes parenting problems caused by difficulties in bonding to surviving infants.

---

\*Statement of Vision and Principles as adopted by participants of the Post-Abortion Summit Conference, Washington DC, 1993.

## II. THE CHURCH'S RESPONSE

A. Post-abortion healing ministry in and of the Church seeks to replicate the life and ministry of Jesus Christ as it recognizes those wounded by abortion and seeks to reconcile them with God, the Church, and themselves. Post-abortion healing ministry is a vital expression of the Church's identity as the Body of Christ.

B. The Catholic Church seeks to encourage and assist all Christians who minister to those damaged by abortion.

C. Specifically, Project Rachel, originating in the United States, is a post-abortion healing and reconciliation ministry of the Catholic Church.

   1. Project Rachel seeks to help heal women, men, siblings, family members, abortion survivors and abortion providers who have been damaged by the experience.

   2. Project Rachel is dedicated to assisting clergy, religious, therapists, and lay people to become more effective in their ministry to victims of abortion.

   3. Project Rachel promotes research into root causes and evaluates results to determine the most effective methods of treatment.

   4. Project Rachel works to raise awareness of the total Church community to their responsibility of leading and supporting victims of abortion during their ongoing healing journey.

   5. Project Rachel is ultimately concerned with spiritual healing. The Sacrament of Reconciliation, integration into the full life of the Church, and spiritual support are all crucial components.

# 3

## The Psychological Realities
## of Induced Abortion

*Vincent M. Rue, Ph.D.*

---

### INTRODUCTION

Examining the psychological impact of induced abortion would seem to be a straightforward task. Embroiled in controversy, elective abortion remains one of the most emotionally charged and politically sensitive topics worldwide. Largely because of this, the emotional aftereffects of elective abortion remain underreported, underestimated, and their remediation undervalued.

Throughout the world, it is estimated that there are some 50 million women who have abortions annually.[1] If the relevant others are included, i.e., the pregnant woman's mate, her parents, and his parents, it is possible that one-half billion people may somehow be touched by this all too common experience. As overwhelming as these figures may be, they are just numbers, figures without faces, procedures without pathos, and symbols without stories.

In the United States, because abortion is selected some 1.6 million times annually, the average American woman has an estimated 46% chance of experiencing an abortion in her lifetime.[2] Even with strong moral opposition to abortion, a recent national survey of American Catholics reported that more than one out of three knew someone who has had an abortion.[3] It may be increasingly difficult to find a home in America in which either a family member or family friend has not had an abortion. According to Steinberg, "with so many millions of women undergoing this life-changing event, we must examine how abortions affect the psyches of these women."[4] In addition to women, others can be significantly impacted, even traumatized: the male partner, grandparents, siblings, friends, future relationships, subsequent children, and health care providers.

5

Given the numbers of individuals potentially affected by abortion, it is surprising how little is known. In the United States, how abortion impacts women and these many individuals is largely speculative. There has never been one large-scale, national, epidemiological study of the psychological effects of induced abortion. Former President Ronald Reagan's chief public health officer, Surgeon General C. Everett Koop, called for such a study in 1987. It was never funded.

## THE CULTURAL CONTEXT OF ABORTION:
The Reality of Private Violence

Both in public policy and in personal decision making, induced abortion does not occur in a cultural vacuum. Instead, abortion exists within a U.S. culture sympathetic to new rules and new expectations concerning personal freedoms and so called "reproductive rights." Given this shift, it appears that the cultural context of induced abortion in the U.S. is predicated upon some fundamental changes: (1) a culture-free independence, i.e., value-freedom versus value-direction; (2) an affirmation of the legitimacy of temporary commitments to others dependent upon the degree of self-enhancement realized; (3) a permanent commitment to self-actualization; and (4) the psychosocial transformation of desires to needs.[5]

In this cultural context, anyone or anything that restricts the acquisition and/or maintenance of a self-actualizing lifestyle can be defined as an impediment and/or burden to be eliminated. Hence, because of the perceived burden of children and the perceived role interference they cause, for American children, born or unborn, a culture of "private violence" is now not only a way of life, but a threat to life.

Private violence is an act of aggression conducted in the privacy of one's home by people who know each other, and even profess to love each other. It stems from a violation of trust and is exercised on those nearest, most vulnerable, and least able or inclined to defend themselves against their attackers.

There is no dispute that the United States is now the most violent nation on earth. More homicides occur here than anywhere else. Hiding under the civility of its vast educational, technological and economic advances, this nation, dedicated to personal freedoms and the primacy of privacy, appears to be pushing itself inside out. Today, young people are more likely to be sexually abused, assaulted physically, or emotionally abused by a family member than a stranger. For children under the age of four, the person most likely to be the most dangerous is their parent.[6] Wives are more likely to be assaulted by their husbands than strangers.[7] There is no place quite so violent now as the American home.[8][9]

This culture of private violence has evolved because of the following factors: (1) the decline of the family;[10] (2) the erosion of traditional values and moral reasoning; (3) the "normalization" of violence, i.e., that abuse and/or death experiences be normative not exceptional; (4) that victims be perceived as less than human and appropriate dehumanizing words and actions be developed and employed; (5) that repeated exposures to abuse and/or death occur with sufficient frequency so as to produce emotional numbness in the individual and indifference in society; (6) that the perpetrators employ justifications rationalizing their violent aggressiveness; (7) that victims become perpetrators in some way to gain mastery over trauma; and (8) that the culture of private violence create and enable an abusive/killing field protected by secrecy, denial and legality and legitimized as expediency, self-empowerment and freedom to choose.

Any attempt to assess and remediate the psychological realities of induced abortion must necessarily take into account this culture of private violence. Elective abortion has both contributed to as well as been impacted by this culture of violence.

## ABORTION: THE REPRODUCTIVE SECRET

The personal context of an unwanted pregnancy is typically one of surprise and failure, surrounded by secrecy and shame. Because of this, denial of ones abortion experience and self-deception regarding post-abortion feelings are common.

According to Lerner, secrecy is a deliberate attempt to conceal that which makes a difference. Today, unexamined deception is threatening our survival far more than enhancing it. In the service of deception, secrecy protects us from the perceived reactions of significant others but ultimately compounds the painful feelings it is meant to deflect.[11]

Secrecy blocks possibility, i.e., the potential for openness, healing, self-acceptance and intimacy.[12] Truth-telling is reliant upon truth-accepting. But if "pretending" is so closely associated with "femininity" as Lerner suggests, deceiving and pretending about abortion for women may be more a cultural imperative than an indication of psychopathology. However, there is an individual and collective price to be paid:

> In so doing, we may also preserve lies that oppress us, rather than lay claim to our individual freedom. In the name of privacy, we withhold from each other our honest experience. We fail to know each other and be known. We fail individually and collectively to scrutinize the "personal" or private ways that would challenge us to seek new truths and revise old ones.[13]

Jung declared that a "lie makes no sense unless the truth is felt to be dangerous." An interesting and perhaps highly unusual research problem has arisen in the examination of the aftereffects of induced abortion. There is considerable evidence that American women are uncomfortable acknowledging whether they have ever had an induced abortion. This reluctance to disclose is evident in relationships with loved ones, friends, pastors, pscyhotherapists, health care providers and researchers.

One possible explanation might be the unanticipated effect of grief. While intensely private in nature, grief is a universal response to loss and/or death. Mourning is the process whereby grief is resolved. When a pregnancy loss as in abortion is traumatic, and cannot be openly acknowledged, publicly mourned or socially supported, the parent lives in isolation. For such an individual, grief is "disenfranchised."[14] But there is also an intrapsychic aspect to the sociological reality of disenfranchised grief, namely, self-disenfranchisement.[15] The interaction between society and the self's disenfranchisement is both cause and effect.

In many cultures, death is an unspeakable loss which generates profound feelings of loss, guilt, shame and grief. Indeed, the defense mechanisms of denial, repression and suppression require and necessitate the maintenance of silence to ward off intrusive feelings of anxiety, pain and stress. It is this same silence that perpetuates self-disenfranchised grief.

According to Kaufman's typology, in self-disenfranchised grief, the individual is responsible for the lack of acknowledgment and acceptance of the painful aftereffects of the loss. The primary psychological factor inhibiting the recognition of feelings of grief is shame. One then is disenfranchised by one's own feelings of shame. It is common for one to feel shame in the face of normal guilt. Shame and its related feelings of alienation and inferiority can be directly attributable to experiences that are defined as "breaking the interpersonal bridge" as discussed by Kaufman. This occurs when

(1) the familiar becomes foreign; (2) others are depersonalized; (3) there is a failure to act in accordance with internalized concepts of responsibility; (4) internalized values are transgressed; (5) trust is broken down; and (6) stigmatization and isolation result.[16] Shame and guilt are clearly principal components of traumatization.[17] If abortion is an intentionally caused human death event, then it is likely that the effects of "breaking the interpersonal bridge" are considerable and psychologically serious.

When guilt is inhibited, it can lead to complicated mourning. Guilt that is unsanctioned and shame-covered in the mourning process will have consequences commonly associated with guilt complications in impacted and pathological grief, i.e., recurrence of the unresolved guilt produces conflicts in other relationships, fears of abandonment, self-destructive behaviors, anger, feelings of inadequacy, and depression. Ashamed of one's behavior and emotions, the individual may experience a disorder of one's sense of self, such as emotional numbing, dissociation, self-alienation, and a damaged sense of egomastery.[18]

Because abortion is an unsanctioned death event, because the decision to terminate the life of one's fetal child is beyond the range of normal human experience, and because abortion can be described as a significant "breaking of the interpersonal bridge," individuals experiencing this procedure may commonly condemn themselves to a life of silence and atonement or denial and fear. Unacknowledged grief and guilt, anticipated condemnation by others, as well as the terror of reexperiencing the trauma all enable and maintain the parameters of secrecy and isolation.

According to Klein, three out of four people surveyed keep sexual secrets, like abortion, from their partners and even sometimes from themselves.[19] By not acknowledging an abortion experience to one's self and/or to one's significant others, a psychological barrier is erected and an emotional toxicity is perpetuated. Coupled with denial, avoidance of abortion-related traumata can occur on a number of levels: (1) avoidance of affect/feelings (numbing); (2) avoidance of knowledge of the event (amnesia); (3) behavioral avoidance (phobic responses); and (4) avoidance of communication about the event (interpersonal distancing).[20]

If abortion is to be accurately understood, its cultural context cannot be ignored. This context largely determines what secrets can be privately acknowledged, what can be discussed, with whom and when. If valid conclusions are to be reached from scientific inquiries about abortions psychosocial sequelae and prevalence, then it is vital that this aspect of reproductive secrecy be acknowledged and addressed in future investigations. If women who have experienced abortion as stressful are to be helped, then disclosure resistance should be presumed and resistance reduction measures should be incorporated into the treatment process, and preabortion counseling protocols.

THE SCIENTIFIC CONTROVERSY:
Does Abortion Carry Significant Psychological Health Risks?

Prior to the legalization of induced abortion in the U.S., many studies identified psychological harm from this procedure. It is unknown what effect illegality played in contributing to post-abortion trauma. However, since the legalization of induced abortion in 1973, advocates of abortion rights have strongly defended the necessity of legal and safe abortion, including minimal emotional risks.

In 1979, Mall and Watts provided the only edited compendium of articles published documenting negative psychological sequelae post-abortion.[21] Later on, more books began addressing the possibility of post-abortion emotional harm and the treatment strategies for recovery: Stanford-Rue, 1986;[22] Speckhard, 1987;[23] Reardon, 1987;[24] Michels, 1988;[25] Crawford and Mannion, 1989;[26] Reisser and Reisser, 1989;[27] Selby, 1990;[28] and Winkler, 1992.[29]

Recent publications in peer-reviewed professional journals have also documented the psychological risks of induced abortion: Rue, 1986;[30] Hittner, 1987;[31] Zakus and Wilday, 1987;[32] Campbell, Franco and Jurs, 1988;[33] Ney and Wickett, 1989;[34] Rogers, Stoms and Phifer, 1989;[35] DeVeber, Ajzenstat and Chisholm, 1991;[36] Rogers, 1991;[37] El-Mallakh and Tasman, 1991;[38] Rue and Speckhard, 1991;[39] Angelo, 1992;[40] Speckhard and Rue, 1992;[41] Franz and Reardon, 1992;[42] and Speckhard and Rue, 1993.[43] Nevertheless, the viewpoint that abortion can cause serious psychological harm for some women is not the prevailing opinion in this country.

The vast majority of professional publications on abortion's emotional aftermath in this country espouse the view that: (1) abortion primarily causes relief; (2) abortion is psychologically safe short-term; (3) the emotional harm some women experience post-abortion is not attributable to the abortion, but to their pre-abortion psychological fragility; (4) abortion is a maturing experience for women; and (5) abortion is an important coping mechanism and is associated with higher levels of self-esteem.[44]

According to Rosenfield, "studies indicate that most women have a sense of relief after abortion, although the next most common emotional response is guilt.[45]

University of Chicago psychiatrist Nada Stotland has boldly asserted to American physicians in the *Journal of the American Medical Association,* "There is no evidence of an abortion trauma syndrome."[46] She goes on to describe this syndrome as a "myth." She is not alone. This position is largely supported by the official committees of the American Psychiatric and Psychological Associations.

There are some 375 studies on the psychological aftereffects of induced abortion. Some are anecdotal, some are reviews, and most are so methodologically flawed as to limit their utility. Nevertheless, both sides of the abortion debate refer to various studies suggesting either the existence or nonexistence of post-abortion sequelae. Pro-abortion Dr. Henry David concluded, "Regardless of personal convictions about abortion, there is general agreement that uncertainty persists about the psychological sequelae of terminating pregnancies."[47]

And yet, in a recent assessment of the aftereffects of abortion, Adler et al. reported that "the weight of the evidence in scientific studies indicates that legal abortion of an unwanted pregnancy in the first trimester does not pose a psychological hazard for most women."[48] Nevertheless, the authors, a panel of experts from the American Psychological Association, acknowledged three confounding problems that severely limit the validity of their own conclusions: (1) "each study has methodological shortcomings and limitations"; (2) "no definitive conclusions can be drawn about longer term effects"; and (3) "women who are more likely to find the abortion experience stressful may be underrepresented in volunteer samples."[49] Even to the most unbiased observer, these limitations would certainly seem to question the validity of making such sweeping claims about the psychological safety of induced abortion at this time.

A widely accepted scientific dictum applies here: poor studies yield poor results. As an example, the American Psychological Association has identified a study by Major et al. as one of the best methodologically designed studies done to date. This study found at both three hours and three weeks after abortion, 85% felt relief and

15% felt moderately to severely depressed.[50] A closer look, however, revealed that despite the short follow-up period, 60% of the research participants dropped out of the study before the three week follow-up evaluation. Hence, the study's conclusions are certainly questionable given the substantial amount of error introduced because of sample attrition.

In the first quasi-prospective national study of the psychological effects of abortion on self-esteem, Russo and Zierk conducted secondary data analysis of a large random sample of American youth (N = 5,295,773 of whom had had an abortion). They concluded that having one abortion was positively associated with higher global self-esteem, particularly feelings of self-worth, capableness, and not feeling one is a failure; they found no evidence of widespread post-abortion traumatization. Further, they asserted, "Insofar as childbearing interferes with access to coping resources, abortion may play important mediating and moderating roles enhancing women's well-being."[51]

Yet even Russo and Zierck caution, "It is important to recognize that some women, particularly women with preexisting emotional problems, are at higher risk for negative emotional responses after abortion than are other women."[52] Unfortunately, the special needs of these women are generally ignored in pre-abortion counseling protocols. Instead of offering special help for these women, if they have problems post-abortion, they are simply blamed for their negative reactions because of their preexisting emotional state. Rather than affirming or assisting, this merely causes revictimization and appears to be a new type of victim-blaming.

If abortion produces higher levels of self-esteem in women who have elected this procedure versus women who have never experienced a pregnancy or abortion, then one would expect women with more abortions to have even higher levels of self-worth. The opposite is in fact the case. Russo and Zierk found that women who had multiple abortions were significantly more likely to agree with this statement: *"I do not have much to be proud of."*[53]

Overall, the findings of Russo and Zierck should be considered suspect due to the methodological weaknesses of investigator bias, their use of secondary data and no direct contact/interviewing with the respondents, the underreporting of the number of women acknowledging they had an abortion, and the overreliance on one forced-choice instrument that was comprised of only 10 statements on which the respondent rated her agreement/disagreement regarding "self-esteem."

The results of Russo and Zierck are contradicted by an equivalent large-scale survey of 612 adults. This study found that among nine possible categories that could contribute to low self-image, abortion was ranked as the highest threat to self-esteem by 67% of women of childbearing age and 55% of men.[54]

In 1989 U.S. Surgeon General Koop reported on his findings after meeting with scientists and clinicians and reviewing over 250 articles pertaining to the health risks of abortion. He wrote on January 9, 1989, "All these studies were reviewed. . . . The data do not support the premise that abortion does or does not cause or contribute to psychological problems." And on March 16, 1989, Dr. Koop testified in the U.S. Congress, "There is no doubt about the fact that there are those people who do have severe psychological problems after abortion" (p. 232). He went on to say, "If you study abortion the way many people have and see how well women feel about their decision three months after the actual procedure, you can be very badly misled" (p. 241).[55]

Most, if not all, recent reviews of the literature corroborate Koop's assessment.[56] (Huckeba and Mueller, 1987; APA, 1987). Rue, Speckhard, Rogers and Franz provided the only empirical assessment of the literature presented to Surgeon General Koop.[57] In this report, Rogers contributed both a meta-analysis and systematic analysis of 239 articles which were reviewed and classified according to research design. Anecdotal and review articles were eliminated, and 13 postpartum control group studies were meta-analyzed. Thirty-two prospective and thirty retrospective uncontrolled studies were systematically analyzed. Of the latter two types of studies, 95% had inadequate sample sizes, 63% had sample attrition, and 74% had unknown or low reliability. Of 19 threats to validity, 4 were found in at least 50% of the studies, 11 in 40% of the studies, 13 in 30% of the studies, and 15 in 20% of the studies.

The median number of methodological shortcomings per uncontrolled study was 7.5. The median sample size was 103 subjects with an attrition rate of 24%. Only 31% used a standardized outcome measure. It was also found that those uncontrolled studies with the greatest methodological weaknesses were more likely to report higher rates of positive experiences after abortion. From his meta-analysis, Rogers demonstrated that post-abortion women demonstrate more psychosocial sequelae than control group women who delivered. A recent meta-analysis conducted by Posavac and Miller concurred that existing research is flawed methodologically and that when compared with women who deliver, women electing abortion tend to show more negative outcomes.[58]

Rue, Speckhard, Rogers and Franz concluded (1) the abortion literature is largely flawed as to design and methodology; (2) that all psychological studies of abortion evidence some negative outcomes for at least a proportion of those women studied; (3) that the clinical literature and experience with post-abortion trauma is more convergent than divergent in the discovery and formulation of post-abortion trauma; and (4) that the type of error found in the many studies examined *underestimates* the negative responses to abortion.

### THE EVIDENCE OF POST-ABORTION EMOTIONAL HARM

Not all women who elect abortion have a traumatic response. Nor is abortion such a benign psychological experience that women should be misinformed about its significant emotional risks for some individuals. The fact is, insufficient scientific data is available in this country to conclude how many women and men are negatively impacted by abortion and which types of individuals are at risk compared to other possible alternatives. Though existing research has identifiable methodological weaknesses, in the aggregate, these studies suggest a direction of harm and a significant percent of individuals likely to be negatively impacted.

In 1993, the Commonwealth Fund commissioned a major survey of American women's health issues. Of 2,210 women interviewed, only 309 (12%) acknowledged having had an abortion, likely a 50% underreporting. Women were asked over the past week how frequently they felt sad, depressed or that they were disliked, had restless sleep, enjoyed life (reverse scored) or had crying spells.[59] While not statistically significant, when compared to women in the general population, women who elected abortion were more likely to report a high degree of depression (45 % v. 39%).[60] Given the tendency of this survey to underreport, this negative trend most likely underestimates the degree of emotional harm and should sound a cautionary note as to the psychological safety of induced abortion.

In Table 1, a synopsis is provided of those nonanecdotal studies which document the existence of post-abortion psychological health risks and injury.

# Table 1.
## Studies Documenting
## the Degree of Post-Abortion Emotional Harm

| Author | Date | Sample Size | Findings of Negative Emotional Sequelae Post-Abortion |
|---|---|---|---|
| Louis Harris Survey on the Health of American Women[60] | 1993 | 2,210 | Women who have experienced an abortion (N = 310) were more likely to be severely depressed (45%) than women in general (39%). |
| Open Arms AIS Project[71] | 1993 | 828 | 27% suicidal<br>81 % lowered self-esteem<br>32% drug/alcohol abuse<br>32% nightmares<br>11% attempted suicide<br>46% despair/helplessness |
| Akron Pregnancy Service[72] | 1993 | 344 | 66% guilt<br>22% nightmares<br>38% lowered self-esteem<br>46% inability to forgive self<br>27% despair/hopelessness<br>54% regret and remorse<br>16% suicidal impulses |
| Russo & Zierck[44] | 1992 | 773 | Women with repeat abortions were significantly more likely to say they did not have much to be proud of and were significantly more likely to wish they had more self-respect. Women with preexisting emotional problems are at higher risk for negative emotional responses after abortion. |
| Gallup Survey[54] | 1992 | 612 | 67% of women and 55% percent of men indicated having an abortion would make them feel very bad about themselves. |
| Hanley et al.[75] | 1992 | 105 | Women who were distressed following an abortion scored significantly higher than the nondistressed group on PTSD symptoms of intrusion and avoidance. |
| Miller[62] | 1992 | 967 | 22% feeling of "sexlessness"<br>18% distress<br>22% significant emotional upset |
| Franz & Reardon[42] | 1992 | 252 | Adolescents were significantly more likely to be dissatisfied with the choice of abortion than adult women, to be dissatisfied with the abortion services, to report being misinformed and to report greater degree of psychological stress. |

## Table 1 (continued)

| Author | Date | Sample Size | Findings of Negative Emotional Sequelae Post-Abortion |
|---|---|---|---|
| Lemkau[78] | 1991 | 63 | 20% felt pre-abortion pressure<br>33% believed they were inadequately prepared for abortion<br>75% received no counseling pre-abortion<br>16% reported problems post-abortion necessitating professional counseling |
| Vaughan[77] | 1991 | 232 | 94% unmarried relationships failed<br>36% suicidal ideation<br>45% negative feelings regarding subsequent pregnancies, problems bonding and/or obsessive thoughts of having a replacement child |
| Barnard[74] | 1990 | 80 | 18% diagnosed post-traumatic stress disorder 3 - 5 years later<br>46% high stress post-abortion reactions (intrusion & avoidance) |
| Campbell et al.[33] | 1988 | 71 | 29% of post-abortion adolescents made suicidal attempts |
| Reardon[24] | 1987 | 252 | 61% flashbacks<br>54% anniversary reactions<br>33% suicidal ideation<br>49% first use or increased use of drugs |
| Hittner[31] | 1987 | 217 | 29% were "not too happy" post-abortion |
| Speckhard[23] | 1987 | 30 | 81 % low self worth<br>69% sexual dysfunction<br>89% preoccupation with aborted child |
| Peppers[69] | 1987 | 80 | There are grief reactions to elective abortion. When compared to involuntary pregnancy loss, the grief scores of women electing abortion was higher (35.45 v. 32.20). Some experience minimal dysfunctional grief reactions while others suffer greatly. |
| Garfinkel, et al.[100] | 1986 | 3,636 | For 202 adolescents who had attempted suicide, an induced abortion was commonly found and statistically associated with a suicidal attempt. Other factors associated: divorce, unemployment, separation, legal difficulties, jail and school suspension. |
| Major,et al.[50] | 1985 | 247 | 15% moderate to severe symptoms of depression |

## Table 1 (continued)

| Author | Date | Sample Size | Findings of Negative Emotional Sequelae Post-Abortion |
|---|---|---|---|
| Bradley[79] | 1984 | 254 | Women with prior abortions described themselves as less well adjusted during a subsequent prenatal period and had lower self-esteem in the postpartum period than those without any abortion history. |
| David, et al.[33] | 1981 | 27,000 | Three months later, women who had aborted were more likely than women delivering to be admitted to a psychiatric hospital (18.4/10,000 v. 12.0/10,000). Women who had aborted were twice as likely as women in general to be admitted for psychiatric hospitalization (18.4 v. 7.5). Women who had aborted and who had no support from significant others were four times as likely to be admitted for psychiatric hospitalization as women who delivered (63.8 v. 16.9). |
| Ashton[133] | 1980 | 109 | Eight weeks post-abortion, 44% complained of nervous disorders, 36% had sleep disorders and 31% had regrets. |
| Freeman[88] | 1980 | 413 | Women who have repeat abortions have significantly higher scores on inter-personal sensitivity, paranoid ideation, phobic anxiety and sleep disturbance to women with one abortion. |

An entire recent issue of the *Journal of Social Issues* examined the psychological effects of elective abortion. Special issue editor Wilmoth concluded, *"There is now virtually no disagreement among researchers that some women experience negative psychological reactions post-abortion."*[61] In that same issue, Wilmoth described Miller's two-year prospective study in San Francisco as the best study to date on abortion's aftereffects. Using a large probability sample of 957 women, Miller asked women who were at a minimum of 60 days post-abortion how they felt. He found 22% reported they felt worse, describing a feeling of "sexlessness" or feeling out of touch with their bodies; at two weeks post-abortion, 38% indicated that they felt relief mixed with feelings of distress with 18% indicating they felt distress only; and 22% reported some significant emotional upset or disturbance after the first few post-abortion weeks.[62] Even more important than these findings, Miller's research has provided preliminary empirical support for the theoretical modeling of pre-abortion decision making and post-abortion loss from a trauma perspective.

Perhaps the best methodologically designed study completed to date is the Denmark study by David, Rasmussen and Holst.[63] Admissions to psychiatric hospitals were tracked for a three-month period after either delivery or abortion for all Danish women under the age of 50 and then compared with the three-month admission rate to psychiatric hospitals for all Danish women of similar age. They found, "As Table 3 shows, at all parities, women who obtained abortions are at higher risk for admission to psychiatric hospitals than are women who delivered" (p. 155). For aborting women, the psychiatric admission rate per 10,000 was 18.4 compared to 12.0 for delivering women, as compared to 7.5 for all Danish women aged 15-49. Even more troublesome are the findings concerning women who are divorced, separated, or widowed at the time of abortion or delivery. The corresponding rates of psychiatric admission are 63.8 per 10,000 for these women aborting versus 16.9 for these women delivering.

Four points require emphasis regarding David's study: (1) the study is relatively short term and provides no long-term assessment of differences between women who abort versus those who deliver; (2) this study most likely underreports the incidence and degree of post-abortion traumatization since women may often be in denial for a considerable period of time after their abortions; (3) the outcome measure utilized was admission to a psychiatric hospital—the worst case circumstance; it would be expected that there would be substantial quantitative differences between these two groups if one used less severe dependent variables like depressive symptomatology or outpatient treatment in psychotherapy; and (4) that women who elected abortion at all ages, parities, and relationship strata (except women aged 35-39, those with 5 pregnancies, and those that were married) had higher rates of admission to psychiatric hospitals than women who delivered.

In Reardon's 1987 exploratory study of high stress post-abortion women, the majority experienced over 28 negative outcomes including the following: flashbacks (61%), anniversary reactions (54%), suicidal ideation (33%), sexual difficulties (59%), feelings of having less control of their lives (78%), difficulty in maintaining and developing relationships (52%), first use or increased use of drugs (49%), and delayed onset of stress with most reporting experience of their worst reactions one year or more post-abortion (62%).[64]

Likewise, Speckhard found that all of the high-stress women in her small descriptive sample had long-term grief reactions, some lasting for over five years.[65] The majority reported feelings of depression (100%), anger (92%), guilt (92%), fears that others would learn of the abortion (89%), preoccupation with the aborted child (81%), feelings of low self worth (81%), discomfort around small children (73%), frequent crying (81%), flashbacks (73%), sexual dysfunction (69%), suicidal thoughts (65%), and increased alcohol usage (61%). The majority of the women studied reported being surprised at such intense reactions to their abortions.

High-stress post-abortive women are doubly stigmatized—first by their reluctance to share their abortion experiences with one another for fear of being viewed as deviant and secondly by feeling that their reactions are a sign of maladjustment to what appears to be a relatively simple, common and benign procedure. Even Former U.S. Surgeon General Koop acknowledged that more than one out of two women in federal reproductive surveys denied ever experiencing an abortion when statistical estimates suggested they had.[66]

Assessing the impact of abortion may not be as simple as some have suggested. In her book entitled *Parental Loss of a Child,* Rando included a chapter on induced abortion, in which Betty Harris reported three obstacles to identifying negative responses following abortion: (1) masking of emotional responses may occur both at the time of the abortion and in later contacts with professionals. If grief persists, it may surface in disguised form and be expressed behaviorally or in psychosomatic complaints; (2) because of the self-insulation associated with the abortion experience, it is important that the caregiver be aware of the potential for grief and take the initiative in exploring the client's perceptions and reactions; and (3) if the caregiver has ambivlent or unresolved feelings about abortion this may interfere with the accurate assessment of post-abortion trauma and the establishment of trust and the ability to be patient and empathic.[67]

Joy reported on the need to be alert to the significant number of women who are requesting counseling for depression resulting from unresolved grief over a prior abortion, i.e., a delayed grief reaction.[68] Peppers confirmed the existence of post-abortion grief occurring irrespective of planning or acceptance of the pregnancy.[69] Several researchers have commented that the reproductive status of women seen in psychiatric outpatient and inpatient settings is often overlooked or not reported. Most importantly, *"a recent abortion or delivery may be buried in a woman's history rather than highlighted as a possible factor in her illness and decision to seek psychiatric care."*[70]

Two recent surveys of women with prior abortions seeking subsequent crisis pregnancy counseling indicate that the percentages of women harmed from abortion could be substantially higher than current studies estimate. In both of these studies the majority of respondents reported post-abortion guilt, regret/remorse, depression, anger/rage, and lowered self-esteem.[71, 72]

In an older study conducted in Britain, Belsey et. al found 64% of the women felt guilty and 61% ambivalent three months post abortion and that those most likely to be disturbed after the abortion had a history of psychosocial instability, poor or no family ties, few friends, and a poor work pattern.[73] This study, the King's Termination Study, provides empirical validation that abortion only worsens an already psychologically unstable situation.

In a very recent study of 984 women randomly selected for follow-back from their abortion, Barnard found approximately 60% gave a wrong phone number at the abortion clinic. Because of this, she was only able to obtain a sample of 80 women. Nevertheless, her findings are important: (1) 68% at the time of the abortion had little to no religious involvement; (2) the sample was normally distributed as to values; (3) three-five years post-abortion, 18% of the sample met the full diagnostic criteria for Post-Traumatic Stress Disorder and 46% displayed high-stress reactions to their abortion.[74] Similar findings were also reported by Hanley et al. in a comparison study of women distressed post-abortion using post-traumatic stress disorder standardized instruments and interviews. They found, *"women who were distressed following an abortion scored significantly higher than the nondistressed group on PTSD symptoms of intrusion and avoidance."*[75]

In a carefully designed recent study, Hanley, Piersma, King, Larson and Foy evaluated whether some women in outpatient mental health treatment with a presenting problem of post-abortion distress met DSM-III-R criteria for the Post-traumatic Stress Disorder (PTSD) categories of intrusion, avoidance, and hyperarousal. 105 women were administered the SCID-PTSD module, the Impact of Event Scale, as well as the Social Support Questionnaire and the Interview for Recent Life Events, in addition to completing a semi-structured interview. The researchers concluded that *"the data from this study are suggestive that women can report abortion-related distress similar to classic PTSD symptoms of intrusion, avoidance and hyperarousal and that these symptoms can be present many years after the abortion."*[76]

Vaughan recently studied 232 women who had obtained abortions. Her purposive sample from 39 states had a mean time post-abortion of 11 years. She found (1) that 67% now had children and 23% avoided trying to conceive; (2) only 5.9% of those not married but in a relationship at the time of the abortion continued their relationships; (3) that worsened interpersonal relationships correlated with higher post-abortion levels of anger and guilt; (4) that 45% had negative feelings regarding subsequent pregnancies, problems bonding and/or obsessive thoughts of having a replacement child; (5) that 24% had medical problems perceived as caused by the abortion; (6) that 28 % had fears of infertility or miscarriage or future fetal anomalies; (7) that 36% had suicidal thoughts; and (8) that 42% reported negative interaction with abortion clinic staff, including finding the staff to be insensitive, cold, impersonal, and being dissatisfied with the abortion counseling.[77]

In a related study, Lemkau found that 20% of her small sample felt pressured in their abortion decision. Most importantly, however, more than one out of three women studied reported that they felt inadequately prepared for the abortion experience. Three out of four women reported receiving no counseling prior to their abortion. Sixteen percent indicated the need for professional counseling afterwards to help them deal with post-abortion problems.[78]

In a Canadian study examining the impact of abortion on subsequent pregnancies, women with a prior abortion reported significantly higher levels of depressive affect in the third trimester of pregnancy and postpartum. The author found women with prior abortions described themselves as less well-adjusted during the prenatal period and had lower self-esteem.[79] Results from this study confirmed the findings of an earlier study by Devore which found that 16% of women with prior abortions reported moderate postpartum depression, with 80% describing "baby blues."[80] Similar findings were reported by Kumar and Robson in a British study of 119 women who previously aborted and were now pregnant again: *"Unresolved feelings of guilt, grief and loss may remain dormant long after an abortion until they are apparently re-awakened by another pregnancy."*[81]

Given the limitations of existing research, it is difficult to accurately assess the incidence of post-abortion psychological sequelae, much less provide any definitive conclusion. Conservative estimates range from 10% and under.[82] Dagg reported a range of 6%-32% with an average of 15%.[83] Others assess a range of 10-50%.[84] Still others suggest the figures are even higher.[85]

Planned Parenthood has affirmed to some degree the need for more and better "post-abortion counseling" to minimize further traumatization from abortion. "Women can have a variety of emotions following an abortion (grief, depression, anger, guilt, relief, etc.) It is important to give her the opportunity to air these feelings and be reassured that her feelings are normal."[86]

Elsewhere, Planned Parenthood has also acknowledged (1) that 10% of women who have abortions will experience depression; (2) that 5% of women are at risk for enduring severe psychiatric disturbances post-abortion; (3) certain women are more likely to experience negative emotional responses post-abortion: women with pre-abortion psychiatric disturbances; those who are ambivalent; women who do not expect to cope well; women who are pressured; those women electing abortion because of genetic fetal defects; women having second-trimester procedures; women obtaining abortions because of contraceptive failure; and women electing abortion in spite of strong religious convictions opposing abortion.[87]

Examining the aftereffects of elective abortion is important for another reason: more women are returning for a second or third or fourth abortion. Repeat abortions now constitute approximately one out of two abortions performed annually (46%). Studies examining the emotional well-being of women who repeatedly elect this procedure suggest they have increased risks for lowered self-esteem, as reported by Russo and Zierck, as well as more disrupted interpersonal relations,[88] and sleep disturbance.[89]

Landy described the woman seeking a repeat abortion as a "problematic" and "unsuccessful" patient for the abortion clinic counselor. Accordingly, "if the woman herself has a sense of failure," then a referral for psychotherapy would be recommended in this counseling protocol.[90] With the high incidence of repeat abortions today, it is unlikely that such referrals are ever made. It is nearly normative now for the typical abortion patient to have already experienced this procedure. After interviewing more than 1,000 women with crisis pregnancies, Fisher cautions that repeat abortions are both an individual and social problem with physical and emotional suffering as well as a strain on medical and counseling resources.[91]

After examining the well-being of 217 women post-abortion, Hittner found one out of three women were "not too happy." She concluded, *"Women, then, may not only display delayed grief, but may feel unhappy and show negative affect as well. These findings raise questions about the belief that only a few women experience post-abortion emotional difficulties. The findings of this study should indicate to mental health counselors that women who choose to have an abortion are more likely to be depressed and lonely than are those in the general population, both before and immediately after the procedure."*[92]

Indeed, women who elect abortion are more likely than non-aborting women to seek out mental health services.[93] A five-year retrospective study in Canada found an eightfold likelihood of necessitated visits to a psychiatrist for women who aborted versus non-aborting women.[94]

Given what is known at this intermediate level of scientific understanding, even the most conservative assessment would conclude that abortion carries certain identifiable and significant psychological health risks. Some individuals are more at risk than others. If anything, numerous studies show it is likely that the degree of post-abortion emotional harm is underestimated.

## ADOLESCENTS AND ABORTION:
A Special Vulnerability

Under the best of circumstances, the developmental tasks of young people 16-22 years of age are fraught with peril. They are trying to form a stable identity, complete school, enter the occupational world, solidify values, and seek mates, etc. These tasks are complex and time and energy consuming.

In the United States, one out of three consumers of abortion is adolescent. These youthful users of abortion are at special risk for post-abortion traumatization because of their developmental vulnerability. In many respects, they are only partly formed, in the process of becoming. Their ego defenses are maturing; their cognitive schemas about the world, others and themselves are in the process of formation, as is their identity. Such a young woman is a cauldron of emotions, ideas and themes waiting to be forged.

Abortion is a force which can invert an adolescent's emotional and moral world, and subvert her normal developmental strivings. An appreciation for altruism, sublimation and personal responsibility may be inverted as well. Consequently, at a time when the development of self-identity and self-esteem are critical, for adolescents an abortion can be harmful to self-image and maturation. Indeed, in her study, Deutsch found that never-pregnant adolescents manifested significantly higher measures of self-esteem than first time and repeat abortion adolescents.[95]

Adolescence is now considered a "risk factor" for post-abortion emotional problems. Existing research suggests that if the abortion issue is not adequately resolved, adolescents may present later in life with problems around sexuality and parenting;[96] that adolescents are more likely to feel pressured into their abortions, report being misinformed in the pre-abortion counseling, report greater severity of psychological stress post-abortion, and are more likely to have second-trimester abortions which in turn carry greater post-abortion psychological risks;[97] adolescents electing abortion are more likely to score lower on self-control post-abortion;[98] adolescents are more likely to be suicidal post-abortion than adult women;[99] a history of abortion is likely to be associated with adolescent suicidal thinking;[100] abortion carries greater risks for negative interpersonal consequences for adolescents than for adult women;[101] the experience of the procedure itself is considered by many adolescents to be stressful and associated with feelings of guilt, depression and a sense of isolation;[102] adolescents may be somewhat more likely than adults to experience negative responses following abortion;[103] and adolescents are generally in need of more counseling and guidance regarding abortion than adult women.[104]

THE EFFECT OF ABORTION ON OTHERS:
Men, Families, Children and Friends

How abortion affects men is even less well documented. Shostak in his interviews with 1,000 American men who escorted their girlfriends for abortions in 18 states in 1984, found the following: (1) abortion is an unrecognized trauma for males which most go through without any help; (2) that men generally hid their stress and feelings in deference to the feelings of their mates; (3) most of the men interviewed felt isolated, angry at themselves and their partners, and fearful of the emotional damage to their partners; and (4) that most men felt "helpless"—"it's a wound you cannot see or feel, but it exists."[105] While women may choose motherhood, in the case of abortion, men may not choose fatherhood.

Researchers Buchanan and Robbins studied 2,533 adolescent males in Texas and found (1) Hispanic men were more distressed if their girlfriends had an abortion than white or black men; and (2) men whose girlfriends had an abortion were more distressed than men who became fathers.[106]

Because men may not openly grieve, male grief reactions to abortion and pregnancy loss may be perceived as minimal. Research by Stinson suggests that men do grieve following pregnancy loss, but that they often deny their grief and internalize their feelings of loss rather than openly express them due to the cultural norm advocating male inexpressiveness. When men do grieve, they tend to express their grief in culturally prescribed "masculine" ways, i.e., anger, aggressiveness, and control. Men typically grieve privately and, because of cultural norms, men's requests for help may go unacknowledged by themselves or in relationships. Some men actually feel more grief and loss after a pregnancy has ended than women. When compared to women, recent assessments suggest that men are more likely to feel despair post-pregnancy loss, including a pervasive sense of hopelessness, one of the signs of chronic grief.[107]

Most unmarried relationships evidence increasing conflict and decline post-abortion. The following disruptions in both unmarried and married relationships are all too common post-abortion: (1) a reduction in the amount and quality of self-disclosing statements; (2) an increase in the use of defensive communicational strategies, e.g., hostility, avoidance; (3) increased partner communication apprehensiveness resulting in a loss of trust and evolving into a closed versus an open system; and (4) a loss of psychospiritual connectedness between the couple, with shame and guilt predominant.

For some unmarried couples whose relationship has dissolved, a prior shared abortion experience can keep them "connected" in the pain and loss. For these individuals, they remain partners in trauma even though the abortion took place years ago. Here the "death imprint" common in trauma may become transformed into a longing for reunion, though not fully realized. This unconscious bid to sustain the relationship may have the following purposes: (1) to "hold onto" their shared aborted child by maintaining some contact with the parent-partner; (2) to preserve the relationship at any cost as a way of compensating for the loss of the child and having "something" as opposed to "nothing"; (3) to self- or other-punish by reengaging in a destructive or futile relationship as atonement for the abortion. Any attempt, however, to reinstitute the relationship is paradoxically thwarted: the greater the desire to reengage an ended relationship, the more likely the re-activation of buried grief and mourning. As unresolved feelings of loss and guilt surface, increased distancing occurs and a decrease in attraction and desire to build intimacy are likely to result.

Unacknowledged and unresolved post-abortion grief may place interpersonal relationships at risk. Mattinson has reported that delayed grief reactions causing interpersonal stress can take many different forms: mild but persistent, or more extreme forms were triggered many years later by a loss of a different nature. Sometimes husbands were more affected than wives.[108] For most men, abortion is a private exercise in powerlessness. Generally, by law they are excluded from participating in the abortion decision making. Because of this, gender equality is not served and relationships are placed at risk.

Abortion also impacts families as well.[109] If the abortion is a family secret, the woman often feels like her relationships with her family members are altered. She may feel depressed, guilty and shame-filled and be less disclosing, or she may attempt to overcompensate and deny any sense of loss by compulsively pretending. She may also avoid extended family gatherings at which pregnant siblings or young nieces or nephews are present. For some, the abortion secret is compelling evidence of their personal unworthiness and inability to ever be loved and accepted for who they are, both within the family and with friends.

Biological grandparents can bear a double burden of loss if their daughter elects an abortion. They not only experience the loss of their grandchild and all the attendant possibilities for love and affection in their life, but they also feel the loss of their daughter or an altered relationship with her because of her distancing after the abortion.

If parents were involved in promoting the abortion decision, afterwards the daughter/son may feel punitive toward them. This may manifest in reduced communication, withdrawal, increased aggressiveness and hostility, and/or a marked increase in dependency and helplessness. Some women have acknowledged such intense hatred for their mothers who encouraged them to abort that they emotionally disowned them. One such young woman who was treated by the author so decompensated that she experienced a psychotic break. She felt so enraged at her mother's insistence on aborting that in her mind she obliterated both her parents from her consciousness and firmly asserted she was an orphan. Others may acquiesce to their mother's control and pressure to abort. After the abortion, the daughter becomes depressed, realizing she can't please her mother and that their relationship is not only unimproved, but worsened.

When an adolescent elects abortion without parental consultation, she must inevitably return to her family context. However, she returns with a secret that shames and emotionally strains her coping abilities. She must employ increased deception to protect her secret and to protect herself from her perceived fears of being found out and condemned by her parents and siblings. The psychological price of secrecy within the family system is well-documented.[110] Within this primary system, the maintenance of a family secret always exacts a profound emotional price from at least one family member.

In the shadows of an abortion secret, children may become especially vulnerable and develop symptoms or acting out behaviors. Here secondary traumatization can be identified. Clinical evidence suggests secondary traumatization in children post-abortion can include intense overinvolvement in the emotional life of the mother, chronic reexperiencing of the abortion trauma, and a prolonged period of denial, anxiety, and emotional numbing. Ney has addressed these factors and described a typology of children held hostage to an aborted sibling: "the haunted child, the bound child, and the substitute child."

For the preschool child who engages in preoperational, egocentric and magical thinking, comprehending the necessary and intentional death of one's younger sibling in abortion is impossible, prompting considerable confusion and anxiety. Children at this stage attempt mastery of the developmental agenda of basic trust and a sense of autonomy. Abortion impedes these development tasks and promotes a sense of mistrust, fear, doubt, guilt and latent or manifest hostility. According to Weiner and Weiner, *"An abortion can be, for the preschooler, a proof of the parents' capacity to be dangerous. In middle class homes, where the hostility may be more heavily veiled, an abortion and its surrounding mystery can be experienced as a concrete violent act."*[112]

For children of school age or older, the ability to understand cause and effect and the consequence of actions is more developed.

Death is seen as irreversible, and they are likely to experience the death of a sibling as personification and attribute external motives for the death. In other words, these children may see their aborted sibling's death as "murder" by either the doctor or the parents. They may also experience considerable survivor guilt. There is also the impeding of the developmental tasks which may inhibit initiative taking and/or promote a sense of insecurity or inferiority.

For the adolescent who is privy to the truth as to why his or her infant sibling or niece or nephew died, the guilt production and role confusion can be considerable, negatively impacting on the developmental task of ego-identity formation and the mastery of impulses. At such a time of particular developmental vulnerability, the abortion decision sends a highly contradictory message to the adolescent regarding the control of aggressive impulses, support and nurturance for the weak, and the value of human life. This in turn can escalate the generation gap by increasing disillusionment and the erosion of parental respect."[113]

The family then is a unique support system where members are made, hurt and healed. Abortion collides with the fundamentals of family life and alters the following: (1) the membership of the family, namely *size*; (2) the feelings and ideas one has about one's self, namely *self-worth*; (3) the ways family members work out conflict and find meaning in life, namely *communication, parental consultation and problem solving*; and (4) the rules family members use for how they should feel and act which impact and are impacted by the family system, namely *honesty, trust and fairness*.

Abortion then never occurs within a relationship vacuum. Whether the abortion is shared or not, many significant others can be impacted. While abortion has been affirmed as an individual's right in this society, legalities are simply insufficient to mitigate or eliminate the importance of the relationship and/or familial context to which an individual must inevitably return. The personal context of an unwanted pregnancy and abortion are important factors to assess beforehand and to rely upon in post-abortion recovery.

## DEFINING POST-ABORTION TRAUMA

If elective abortion is nothing more than the removal of nondescript cells or tissue, then it would be highly unlikely that such a procedure could cause any significant psychological harm. On the other hand, if elective abortion is an intentionally caused human death experience, then it is likely that some women, men and significant others could manifest profound symptoms of depression, grief and loss.

The essential characteristics of a traumatic event generally include but are not restricted to (1) a serious threat to one's life; (2) a serious threat to one's physical integrity; (3) a serious threat or possible harm to one's children/spouse/close relative/friends; (4) sudden destruction of one's home/community; (5) seeing another person who has been/is being/has recently been seriously injured or killed; (6) physical violence; and (7) learning about serious threat/harm to relative/family.[114]

If abortion is experienced as traumatic, the symptomatic responses may be many and varied. They can include guilt, shame, depression, grief, anxiety, helplessness, hopelessness, sadness, sorrow, lowered self-esteem, distrust, hostility toward self and others, regret, sleep disorders, recurring distressing dreams, nightmares, anniversary reactions, psycho-physiological symptoms, suicidal ideation and behavior, alcohol and/or chemical dependencies and abuse, sexual dysfunction, insecurity, emotional numbing, painful unwanted reexperiencing of the abortion, relationship disruption, communication impairment and/or restriction, isolation, fetal fantasies, self-condemnation, flashbacks, uncontrollable weeping, eating disorders, preoccupation, memory and/or concentration disruption, confused and/or distorted thinking, delusions, dissociations, bitterness, an enduring sense of loss, survivor guilt with an inability to forgive oneself, psychological distress associated with physical complications, and the corresponding increased need for psychotherapeutic and/or psychopharmacological treatment.

The varying manifestations of post-abortion trauma make an accurate assessment of the nature and degree of harm from this procedure all the more important. Too often secondary symptoms become the primary diagnosis with no exploration of a prior induced abortion as causative or problematic.[115] For the clinician unfamiliar with post-abortion trauma, accurate diagnosis and effective treatment are most unlikely.

The American Psychiatric Association (1987) in its *Diagnostic and Statistic Manual of Mental Disorder: DSM-III-R* describes abortion as a type of "psychosocial stressor" (p. 20). Psychosocial stressors can precipitate any number of psychiatric disorders. Abortion as a psychosocial stressor may lead to mild distress or severe trauma creating a continuum of harm with accompanying symptoms ranging from Post-Abortion Distress (PAD) to Post- Abortion Syndrome (PAS) to Post-Abortion Psychosis (PAP). According to Wilmoth, PAS is in the formative stages of conceptualization and operationalization.[116] It took the American Psychiatric Association over a decade to officially recognize Post-Traumatic Stress Disorder. Post-Abortion Distress, Post-Abortion Syndrome and Post-Abortion Psychosis may well be making a similar transition, as none are currently recognized in the *DSM-III-R*.[117]

*Post-Abortion Distress* (PAD) is the manifestation of symptoms of discomfort following an abortion which results from three aspects: (1) the perceived physical pain and emotional stress of the pregnancy and abortion; (2) the perception of a loss from the abortion (i.e., loss of a role, dream, relationship, parts or perception of self, potential life, etc.); (3) the conflict in personality, roles, values and relationships that results from a changed perception of the appropriateness of the abortion decision. PAD may be categorized as an Adjustment Disorder when impairment in occupational functioning or in usual social activities occurs. As such, the onset of distress must occur within three months of the abortion and persist no longer than six months, and persistent reexperience of the abortion stressor cannot be present."[118]

*Post-Abortion Syndrome* (PAS), by definition then, is a type of Post-Traumatic Stress Disorder that is characterized by the chronic or delayed development of symptoms resulting from impacted emotional reactions to the perceived physical and emotional trauma of abortion.

According to the *DSM-III-R* (APA, 1987), Post-Traumatic Stress Disorder traumata involve "an event that is outside the range of usual human experience . . . e.g. serious threat to one's life or physical integrity; serious threat or harm to one's children . . . or seeing another person who has been or is being seriously injured or killed as the result of . . . physical violence" (APA, 1987, 250).

There are four basic components of PAS: (1) exposure to or participation in an abortion experience, i.e., the intentional destruction of one's unborn child, which is perceived as sufficiently traumatic and beyond the range of usual human experience; (2) uncontrolled negative reexperiencing of the abortion death event, e.g. flashbacks, nightmares, grief and anniversary reactions; (3) unsuccessful attempts to avoid or deny abortion recollections and emotional pain which result in reduced responsiveness with others and one's environment; and (4) experiencing associated symptoms not present before the abortion including guilt about surviving."[119]

The diagnostic criteria for PAS are provided in Figure 1. Spontaneous recovery from PAS is not characteristic. While PAS is categorized as a type of PTSD, additional diagnoses including Anxiety, Depressive or Organic Mental Disorder may concurrently be made. Other variants of PTSD, not dissimilar to PAS, are "Rape Trauma Syndrome," "Battered Wives Syndrome," and "Post-Hysterectomy Syndrome," all of which are also not included in the *DSM-III-R,* but which are widely accepted.

More than an accidental grab bag of isolated symptoms, Post-Abortion Syndrome (PAS) is a clustering of related and unsuccessful attempts to assimilate and gain mastery over the abortion trauma. The resulting lifestyle changes involve partial to total cognitive restructuring, behavioral reorganization, and emotional disruption.

*Post-Abortion Psychosis* (PAP) is suggested as a generic designation for major affective or thought disorders not present before an abortion, and directly and clinically attributable to the induced abortion. PAP is characterized by chronic and severe symptoms of disorganization and significant personality and reality impairment, including hallucinations, delusions, and severe depression. Decompensation occurs when the individual becomes aware of, overwhelmed by, and unable to communicate the feelings of guilt, grief, fear, anger, and responsibility for the traumatic death of her/his unborn child. Other manifestations may include intolerable levels of affect, self-condemnation, anxiety, and terror at feeling unable to face the trauma, and also paranoia about being found out. Although PAP is not a commonly encountered reaction to abortion traumatization, clinical evidence of it has been reported.[120]

## PREDISPOSING FACTORS FOR POST-ABORTION TRAUMA

After experiencing a traumatic event, some individuals are more likely than others to develop problems. This is particularly true with respect to induced abortion. A number of risk factors have been identified as predisposing.[121] The possibility of future childlessness because of a previous induced abortion can also be haunting. For others, especially after continued reproductive failures, they live in dread and sadness over the increasing likelihood that they may never be able to have a healthy baby.[122]

## Figure 1: Post-Abortion Syndrome: Diagnostic Criteria*

A. *Stressor:* The abortion experience, i.e., the intentional destruction of one's unborn child, is sufficiently traumatic and beyond the range of usual human experience so as to cause significant symptoms of reexperience, avoidance, and impacted grieving.

B. *Reexperience:* The abortion trauma is reexperienced in one of the following ways:

1. Recurrent and intrusive distressing recollections of the abortion experience;
2. Recurrent distressing dreams of the abortion or of the unborn child (e.g., baby dreams or fetal fantasies);
3. Sudden acting or feeling as if the abortion were recurring, (including reliving the experience, illusions, hallucinations, and dissociative (flashback) episodes including upon awakening or when intoxicated;
4. Intense psychological distress at exposure to events that symbolize or resemble the abortion experience (e.g., clinics, pregnant mothers, subsequent pregnancies);
5. Anniversary reactions of intense grieving and/or depression on subsequent anniversary dates of the abortion or on the projected due date of the aborted child.

C. *Avoidance:* Persistent avoidance of stimuli associated with the abortion trauma or numbing of general responsiveness (not present before the abortion), as indicated by at least three of the following:

1. Efforts to avoid or deny thoughts or feelings associated with the abortion;
2. Efforts to avoid activities, situations or information that might arouse recollections of the abortion;
3. Inability to recall the abortion experience or an important aspect of the abortion (psychogenic amnesia);
4. Markedly diminished interest in significant activities;
5. Feeling of detachment or estrangement from others;
6. Withdrawal in relationships and/or reduced communication;
7. Restricted range of affect, e.g., unable to have loving or tender feelings;
8. Sense of foreshortened future, e.g., does not expect to have a career, marriage, or children, or a long life.

(*continued next page*)

D. *Associated Features:* Persistent symptoms (not present before the abortion), as indicated by at least two of the following:
1. Difficulty falling or staying asleep;
2. Irritability or outbursts of anger;
3. Difficulty concentrating;
4. Hypervigilence;
5. Exaggerated startle response to intrusive recollections or reexperiencing of the abortion trauma;
6. Physiologic reactivity upon exposure to events or situations that symbolize or resemble an aspect of the abortion (e.g., breaking out in a profuse sweat upon a pelvic examination or hearing vacuum pump sounds);
7. Depression and suicidal ideation;
8. Guilt about surviving when one's unborn child did not;
9. Self devaluation and/or an inability to forgive one's self;
10. Secondary substance abuse.

E. *Course:* Duration of the disturbance (symptoms in B, C, and D) of more than one month's duration, or onset may be delayed (greater than six months after the abortion).

*Developed by Vincent M. Rue, Ph.D., from diagnostic criteria for "post-traumatic stress disorder," American Psychiatric Association *Diagnostic and Statistical Manual of Mental Disorders Revised,* (DSM-III-R: 309.89). Washington D.C. American Psychiatric Press, 1987, 250. The American Psychiatric Association in no way supports the existence of, nor does it find any clinical evidence for the basis of the diagnosis of "post-abortion syndrome." The *DSM-III-R* does not reference nor include the diagnosis of "post-abortion syndrome." However, the *DSM-III-R* does identify abortion as a type of "psychosocial stressor" (p. 20).

Frederick contends that post-traumatic stress reactions are more persistent after an event for which human beings are perceived to be responsible.[123] For women who have elected abortion, the volitional nature of their loss may place them at special risk for traumatization as opposed to women who experienced stillbirth or miscarriage, over which they had no control.

Increasing evidence suggests that certain individuals are likely to be highly stressed and/or traumatized post-abortion when the following risk factors are present:[124]

1. Prior history of mental illness;[125,126]
2. Immature interpersonal relationships;
3. Unstable, conflicted relationship with ones partner;[127]

4. History of a negative relationship with one's mother;
5. Ambivalence regarding abortion;[128]
6. Religious or cultural background hostile to abortion;[129]
7. Single status, especially if one has not borne children;
8. Age, particularly adolescents versus adult women;[130]
9. Second-trimester v. first trimester abortions;[131]
10. Abortion for genetic reasons, i.e., for fetal anomaly;[132]
11. Pressure or coercion to abort;[133]
12. Prior abortion(s);[134]
13. Prior children;
14. Maternal orientation;[135]
15. Biased pre-abortion counseling.[136]

There is also evidence that an individual experiencing an abortion is more likely to be traumatized if she believes that the procedure is absolutely safe psychologically. Events need to be given meaning before they are experienced as stressful or not.[137] When the above risk factors are not evaluated prior to abortion, when a woman is led to believe that there are no psychological aftereffects of abortion, and when abortion counseling is deficient, the result is uninformed consent.[138] This comes about when pre-abortion counseling is either not provided, or when it is not process-oriented counseling but simply decision-expediting, impulse- and fear-oriented, lacking in sufficient time and information, not conducted by trained professionals, and sited at an abortion clinic.

If post-abortion trauma is to be prevented, a thorough reassessment of the pre-abortion experience must occur. Appropriate legislation safeguarding a woman's right to know and be fully informed is essential; certification for abortion or crisis pregnancy counseling is necessary; and more complete information regarding fetal development, real alternatives, and the psychological sequelae must be provided.

Lastly, if women are to be adequately informed about significant psychological health risks of abortion, then the information shared with them must be as complete and reliable as possible. Hence, large-scale retrospective and prospective research efforts are needed to examine how women and men cope with their abortion experiences. To pretend that all the necessary data has been collected, that the evidence of the safety of abortion is final and conclusive, and that no further study is required is harmful to the public health of women. When overstatements masquerade as science, both the public and science are harmed.

CONCLUSION

The physical and emotional health of women demands more and better research on this issue, particularly since abortion has become the most common surgical procedure in the U.S. and in many nations throughout the world. Regrettably the prevailing opinion about the psychological aftermath of abortion, as espoused by most national mental health professional associations, is in fact based upon methodologically flawed and substandard studies. These associations factually assert abortion causes no lasting or significant emotional health risks. Because this opinion is based on methodologically weak studies, logically, no conclusive statements about the psychological positive effects of abortion should be accepted at this time.

From a public health perspective, public proclamations about the psychological safety of abortion simply cannot be made with any scientific certitude now. A recent U.S. national task force on women and depression (1990) has issued its final report and lends credence to this position: "Abortion's relative risk of mental disorder compared with other reproductive events has not been fully ascertained."[139]

In the emotionally charged public debate about abortion, overstatements abound. Some claim abortion is psychologically devastating to most.[140] Others claim that there is no evidence whatsoever of any post-abortion trauma.[141]

Rhetoric aside, honest scientific and clinical discourse converges and confirms that there are women and men who are psychologically harmed from their abortion experiences. These individuals need compassion, understanding, and genuine assistance, not judgment, disbelief and stigmatization.

If scientific integrity and genuine compassion for women's health and safety are more than rhetoric, then it is no longer relevant to debate the existence of post-abortion trauma. Rather the concerns should appropriately shift now to (1) how many women and men are affected and to what degree; (2) what refinements are needed in the clinical definitions of post-abortion trauma to improve early diagnosis and treatment; (3) what treatments are most effective in helping which type of distressed persons; (4) what changes in counseling services and public policies need revision to prevent future traumatization from abortion; and (5) what positive and proactive roles can the family, schools, churches and other supportive institutions provide in preventing post-abortion trauma and aiding in the recovery process.

## NOTES

1. International Planned Parenthood Federation. (1992). *Annual Report 1991-92.* London: IPPF, 27.
2. Forrest, J. (1987). "Unintended Pregnancy Among American Women." *Family Planning Perspectives,* 19:76-77.
3. Princeton Survey Research Associates. (1993). "Newsweek Poll of Catholics, August 3-5, 1993." *Newsweek* (August 16).
4. Steinberg, T. (1989). "Abortion Counseling: To Benefit Maternal Health." *American Journal of Law & Medicine* 15:4:483.
5. See: Yankelovich, D. (1981). *New Rules.* New York: Random House.
6. Christoffel, J. & H. Liu, (1983). "Homicide Death Rates in Childhood in 23 Developed Countries: U.S. Rates Atypically High." *Child Abuse & Neglect,* 7, 339-348.
7. Tanay, K. (1984). "Family Violence." *Journal of Forensic Science,* 29, 820-835.
8. For a more complete exposition of violence and the family, see: Rue, V. (1985). "Death by Design of Handicapped Newborns: The Family's Role & Response." *Issues in Law & Medicine,* 1:3:201-225.
9. See also: Ney, P. (1979). "The Relationship Between Abortion and Child Abuse." *Canadian Journal of Psychiatry,* 24:610-620; Ney, P. (1992). "Transgenerational Triangles of Abuse: A Model of Family Violence." *Intimate Violence: Interdisciplinary Perspectives.* Edited by E. Viano. Washington: Hemisphere Publishing, 15-25.
10. Popenoe, D. (1993). "American Family Decline." *Journal of Marriage and the Family,* 55:527-555.
11. Lerner, H.G. (1993). *The Dance of Deception: Pretending and Truth-Telling in Womens Lives.* New York: Harper Collins.
12. Ibid, 38-40.
13. Ibid, 45.
14. Doka, K. (1989). *Disenfranchised Grief.* Lexington, MA: Lexington Books.
15. Kauffman, J. (1989). "Intrapsychic Dimensions of Disenfranchised Grief." *Disenfranchised Grief.* Edited by K. Doka. Lexington, MA: Lexington Books, 25-42.
16. Ibid, 26-29.
17. Wong, M. & D. Cook, (1992). "Shame and Its Contribution to PTSD." *Journal of Traumatic Stress,* 5:4:557-562.
18. Kaufman (1989) 27.
19. Klein, M. (1987). "Sexual Secrets." Paper presented at the annual meeting of the Society for the Scientific Study of Sex, Beverly Hills, CA.
20. See generally: Peterson, K., M. Prout, & R. Schwarz, (1991). *Post-Traumatic Stress Disorder: A Clinician's Guide.* New York: Plenum Press.
21. Mall, D. & W. Watts, (1979). *The Psychological Aspects of Abortion.* Washington, DC: University Publications of America.

22. Stanford-Rue, S. (1986). *Will I Cry Tomorrow? Healing Post-Abortion Trauma*. Fleming, NJ: Revell.
23. Speckhard, A. (1987). *Psycho-Social Stress Following Abortion*. Kansas City, MO: Sheed & Ward.
24. Reardon, D. (1987). *Aborted Women: Silent No More*. Westchester, IL: Crossway.
25. Michels, N. (1988). *Helping Women Recover from Abortion*. Minneapolis, MN: Bethany.
26. Crawford, D. & M. Mannion, (1989). *Psycho-Spiritual Healing After Abortion*. Kansas City, MO: Sheed & Ward.
27. Reisser, T. & P. Reisser, (1989). *Help for the Post-Abortion Woman*. Grand Rapids, MI: Zondervan.
28. Selby, T. (1990). *The Mourning After: Help for Post-Abortion Syndrome*. Grand Rapids, MI: Baker.
29. Winkler, K. (1992). *When the Crying Stops: Abortion. the Pain and the Healing*. Milwaukee, WI: Northwestern.
30. Rue, V. (1986). "Abortion in Relationship Context." *International Review of Natural Family Planning*, 19:2:95-121.
31. Hittner, A. (1987). "Feelings of Well-Being Before and After an Abortion." *American Mental Health Counselors Association Journal*, 9:2:98-104.
32. Zakus, G. & S. Wilday, (1987). "Adolescent Abortion Option." *Social Work in Health Care*, 12:4:77-91.
33. Campbell, N., K. Franco, & S. Jurs, (1988). "Abortion in Adolescence." *Adolescence*, 23:92:813-823.
34. Ney, P. & A Wickett, (1989). "Mental Health & Abortion: Review & Analysis." *Psychiatric Journal of the University of Ottawa*, 14:506-516.
35. Rogers, J., G. Stoms, & J. Phifer, (1989). "Psychological Impact of Abortion." *Health Care for Women International*, 10:347-376.
36. DeVeber, L., J. Ajzenstat, & D. Chisholm, (1991). "Postabortion Grief: Psychological Sequelae of Induced Abortion." *Humane Medicine*, 7:203-209.
37. Rogers, J. (1991). "Utilization of Data in the Ongoing Public Debate Over Abortion." *Family Perspective*, 25:3:179-199.
38. El-Mallakh, R. & A. Tasman, (1991). "Recurrent Abortions in a Bulimic: Implications Regarding Pathogenesis." *International Journal of Eating Disorders*, 10:2:215-219.
39. Rue, V. & A. Speckhard, (1991). "Post-Abortion Trauma: Incidence & Diagnostic Considerations." *Medicine & Mind*, 6:1:57-74.
40. Angelo, E.J. (1992). "Psychiatric Sequelae of Abortion: The Many Faces of Post-Abortion Grief." *Linacre Quarterly*, 59:2:69-80.
41. Speckhard, A. & V. Rue, (1992). "Post-abortion Syndrome: An Emerging Public Health Concern." *Journal of Social Issues*, 42:3:95-119.

42. Franz, W. & D Reardon, (1992). "Differential Impact of Abortion on Adolescents & Adults." *Adolescence,* 27:105:162-172.
43. Speckhard, A. & V. Rue, (1993). "Complicated Mourning & Abortion." *Journal of Pre- and Peri-natal Psychology,* in press.
44. See: Russo, N. & K. Zierk, (1992). "Abortion, Childbearing and Women's Well-Being." *Professional Psychology: Research & Practice,* 23:4:269-280; Dagg, P. (1991). "The Psychological Sequelae of Therapeutic Abortion." *American Journal of Psychiatry,* 148:5:578-585; Armsworth, M. (1991). "Psychological Response to Abortion." *Journal of Counseling & Development,* 69:377-379; Zolese, G. & C. Blacker, (1992). "The Psychological Complications of Therapeutic Abortion." *British Journal of Psychiatry,* 160:742-749; Adler, N., H. David, B. Major, S. Roth, N. Russo, G. Wyatt, (1992). "Psychological Factors in Abortion." *American Psychologist,* 47:10:1194-1204; and Wilmoth, G., de Alteriis, & D. Bussell, (1992). "Prevalence of Psychological Risks Following Legal Abortion in the U.S.: Limits of the Evidence." *Journal of Social Issues,* 48:3:37-66.
45. Rosenfeld, J. (1992). "Emotional Responses to Therapeutic Abortion." *American Family Physician,* 45:1:137-140, 137.
46. Stotland, N. (1992). "The Myth of the Abortion Trauma Syndrome." *Journal of the American Medical Association,* 268:15:2078-2079.
47. David, H. "Post-Abortion Syndrome?" *Abortion Research Notes* (December, 1987) 16:3:1.
48. Adler, N. et al. "Psychological Responses After Abortion" *Science,* (April, 1990), 41-43.
49. Ibid. 42-43.
50. Major, B. et al. (1985). "Attributions, Expectations and Coping with Abortion," *Journal of Personality & Social Psychology,* 48:3:585-599.
51. Russo & Zierk, (1992) 279; See also, Adler, N. et al.
52. Russo & Zierk, (1992) 269.
53. Russo & Zierk, (1992) 274.
54. Gallup Poll (1992). *Newsweek.* (February 17).
55. Koop, C. (1989) Testimony before the Human Resources and Intergovernmental Relations Subcommittee, U.S. House of Representatives. One Hundred First Congress, First Session, Washington, D.C., March 16.
56. Huckeba, W. & C. Mueller, (1987). "Systematic Analysis of Research on Psycho-social Effects of Abortion Reported in Refereed Journals, 1966-1985," Unpublished research monograph, Washington, D.C.: Family Research Council.
57. Rue, V., A. Speckhard, J. Rogers, & W. Franz, (1987)."The Psychological Aftermath of Abortion: A White Paper." Presented to the Office of the Surgeon General, Department of Health & Human Services, Washington, D.C.

58. Posavac, E. & T. Miller, (1990). "Some Problems Caused by Not Having a Conceptual Foundation for Health Research: An Illustration from Studies of the Psychological Effects of Abortion." *Psychology & Health,* 5:13-23.
59. These items were taken from the Center for Epidemiological Studies Depression Scale, *Applied Psychological Measurement,* 1997.
60. Louis Harris & ASSQC. (April 20, 1993). "The Health of American Women." Commissioned by the Commonwealth Fund, Table 418, p. 451. Used with permission.
61. Wilmoth, G. (1992). "Abortion, Public Health Policy, and Informed Consent Legislation." *Journal of Social Issues,* 48:3:1-17, 5.
62. Miller, W. (1992). An Empirical Study of the Psychological Antecedents and Consequences of Induced Abortion. *Journal of Social Issues,* 48:67-94.
63. David, H. N. Rasmussen, & E. Holst, (1981). "Postpartum and Postabortion Psychotic Reactions." *Family Planning Perspectives,* 13:88-91.
64. Reardon, D. (1987). *Aborted Women: Silent No More.* Chicago, IL: Loyola University Press.
65. Speckhard, A. (1987). *Psycho-social Stress Following Abortion.* Kansas City, Sheed & Ward.
66. Koop (1989).
67. Harris, B. (1986). "Induced Abortion." in T. Rando (ed.) *Parental Loss of a Child.* Champaign, IL: Research Press, 241-256.
68. Joy, S. (1985). "Abortion: An Issue to Grieve?" *Journal of Counseling & Development,* 63:6:375-376.
69. Peppers, L. (1987) "Grief and Elective Abortion: Breaking the Emotional Bond?" *Omega* 18:1:1-12.
70. Stotland, N. (1991). *Psychiatric Issues in Abortion,* Washington, DC: American Psychiatric Press, 9.
71. Open Arms. (1993). *Abortion Information Survey Project,* Columbia, MO: P.O. Box 1056.
72. Akron Pregnancy Service. (1993). *Post-Abortion Research Project.* Akron, OH: 105 E. Market St.
73. Belsey, E. et al. (1977) "Predictive Factors in Emotional Response to Abortion: Kings Termination Study - IV." *Social Science & Medicine* 11:71-82.
74. Barnard, C. (1990). *The Long Term Psychosocial Effects of Abortion.* Portsmouth, NH: Institute for Abortion Recovery & Research.
75. Hanley, D. et al. (1992). "Women Outpatients Reporting Continuing Post-Abortion Distress: A Preliminary Inquiry." Paper presented at the annual meeting of the International Society for Post-Traumatic Stress Studies, Los Angeles, CA.
76. Hanley, D., H. Piersma, D. King, D. Larson, & D. Foy, (1992, October 23). "Women outpatients reporting continuing post-abortion distress:

A preliminary inquiry." Paper presented at the Eighth Annual Meeting of the International Society for Traumatic Stress Studies, Los Angeles.
77. Vaughan, H. (1991). *Canonical Variates of Post Abortion Syndrome.* Portsmouth, NH: Institute for Abortion Recovery & Research.
78. Lemkau, J. (1991). "Post-abortion Adjustment of Health Care Professionals in Training." American Journal of Orthopsychiatry, 61:1:92-102.
79. Bradley, C. (1984). "Abortion and Subsequent Pregnancy." *Canadian Journal of Psychiatry,* 29:494.
80. Devore, N. (1979). "The Relationship Between Previous Elective Abortions and Postpartum Depressive Reactions." *Journal of Obstetric Gynecologic Neonatal Nursing,* July/August, 237-240.
81. Kumar, R. & K. Robson, (1978). "Previous Induced Abortion and Ante-Natal Depression in Primiparae: Preliminary Report of a Survey of Mental Health in Pregnancy." *Psychological Medicine,* 8:711-715.
82. See Adler et al. (1990).
83. Dagg, P. (1991). "The Psychological Sequelae of Therapeutic Abortion—Denied and Completed." *American Journal of Psychiatry,* 148:5:578-585 (Table 2).
84. Lodl, K., A. McGettigan, & J. Bucy, (1985) "Women's Responses to Abortion" *Journal of Social Work & Human Sexuality* 3:119-132.
85. Reardon, *op cit.,* (1989).
86. Saltzman, L. & M. Policar, (1985). *The Complete Guide to Pregnancy Testing & Counseling.* San Francisco: Planned Parenthood of Alameda/San Francisco, 94.
87. Planned Parenthood Federation of America. (1993). "The Emotional Effects of Induced Abortion." *Fact Sheet,* New York: 1-6.
88. Freeman, E., K. Rickels & G. Huggins, (1980). "Emotional Distress Patterns Among Women Having First or Repeat Abortions." *Obstetrics & Gynecology,* 55:5:625-635.
89. Berger, C., D. Gold, D. Andres, P. Gillett, & R. Kinch, (1984). "Repeat Abortion: Is it a Problem?" *Family Planning Perspectives,* 16:2:70-75.
90. Landy, U. (1986). "Abortion Counseling: A New Component of Medical Care." *Clinics in Obstetrics and Gynecology,* 13:1:33-42, 40.
91. Fisher, S. (1986). "Reflections on Repeated Abortions: The Meanings and Motivations." *Journal of Social Work Practice,* 2:2:70-87.
92. Hittner, A. (1987). "Feelings of Well-Being Before and After an Abortion." *American Mental Health Counselors Association Journal,* 2:98-104, 102 & 103.
93. Ashton, J. (1980). "The Psychosocial Outcome of Induced Abortion," *British Journal of Obstetrics & Gynecology,* 87:1115-1122.
94. Badgley et al. (1977). *Report of the Committee on the Operation of the Abortion Law.* Ottawa: Supply and Services, 313-321.
95. Deutsch, M. (1982). Personality Factors, Self-Concept, and Family Variables Related to First Time and Repeat Abortion-Seeking Behavior in

Adolescent Women." Unpublished Doctoral Dissertation, Washington, D.C.: American University.

96. Zakus & Wilday (1987).
97. Franz & Reardon (1992).
98. Falk, R., M. Gispert & D. Baucom, (1981), "Personality Factors Related to Black Teenage Pregnancy & Abortion," *Psychology of Women Quarterly,* 5:5:737-746
99. Campbell, Franco & Jurs (1988).
100. Garfinkel, B. et al. (1986). "Stress, Depression and Suicide: A Study of Adolescents in Minnesota." *Responding to High Risk Youth,* Minnesota Extension Service: Univesity of Minnesota.
101. Marecek, J. (1986). "Consequences of Adolescent Childbearing and Abortion." *Adolescent Abortion: Psychological & Legal Issues.* Edited by G. Melton. Lincoln, NE: University of Nebraska Press, 6-115.
102. Biro, F., L. Wildey, P. Hillard & J. Rauh, (1986). "Acute and Long-Term Consequences of Adolescents Who Choose Abortions." *Pediatric Annals,* 15:10:667-672.
103. Adler, N. (1992). "Unwanted Pregnancy and Abortion: Definitional and Research Issues." *Journal of Social Issues,* 48:3:19-35.
104. Gold, J. (1989). "Adolescents and Abortion." *Psychiatric Aspects of Abortion.* Edited by N. Scotland. Washington, DC: American Psychiatric Press, 187-195.
105. Shostak, A. et al. (1984). *Men and Abortion: Lessons. Losses & Love,* New York: Praeger.
106. Buchanan, M. & C. Robbins, (April 18, 1988). "Early Adult Psychological Consequences for Males of Adolescent Pregnancy and Its Resolution." Paper presented at the North Central Sociological Association Annual Meeting, Pittsburgh, PA.
107. Stinson, R. et al. (1992). "Parents' Grief Following Pregnancy Loss: A Comparison of Mothers and Fathers." *Family Relations,* 41:218-223.
108. Mattinson, J. "The Effects of Abortion on a Marriage." Ciba Foundation Symposium, London, 115, 165-177.
109. See for example: Rue, V. (1985). "Abortion in Relationship Context." *International Journal of Natural Family Planning,* 9:95-121.
110. See for example: Webster, H. (1991). *Family Secrets.* Reading, MA: Addison-Wesley Publishing Co.; Imber-Black, E. (1993). *Secrets in Families and Family Therapy.* New York: Norton.
111. Ney, P. (1982). "A Consideration of Abortion Survivors," *Child Psychiatry in Human Development,* 13:168-179
112. Weiner, A. & E. Weiner, (1984). "The Aborted Sibling Factor." *Clinical Social Work Journal,* 34:209-215.
113. See generally: Rue, V. (1985). "Death by Design of Handicapped Newborns: The Family's Role & Response." *Issues in Law & Medicine,* 1:3:201-225.

114. Peterson, K., M. Prout & R. Schwarz, (1991). *Post-Traumatic Stress Disorder: A Clinician's Guide.* New York: Plenum, 15.
115. For additional explanation, see Angelo, J. (1992). "Psychiatric Sequelae of Abortion: The Many Faces of Post-Abortion Grief." *Linacre Quarterly,* 59:2:69-80.
116. Wilmoth, G. (1988) "Depression and Abortion: A Brief Review." *Population & Environmental Psychology News* 14:1:9-12.
117. For additional discussion of post-abortion trauma and its clinical manifestations, see Speckhard, A. & V. Rue, (1992).
118. Speckhard & Rue (1992).
119. Ibid.
120. See: Sim, M. & R. Neisser, (1979). "Predicting the Psychological Consequences of Abortion." *Social Science & Medicine,* 13:683-689; and Spaulding, J. & J. Cavenar, (1978). "Psychoses Following Therapeutic Abortion." *American Journal of Psychiatry,* 135:364-365.
121. Rue, V. & A. Speckhard, (1991). "Post-abortion Trauma: Incidence & Diagnostic Considerations." *Medicine & Mind,* 6:1:57-74
122. Costello, *et. al.* (1988).
123. Frederick, C. (1980). Effects of Natural Versus Human-Induced Violence Upon Victims. *Evaluation and Change* (Special Issue), 71-75.
124. See generally Major, B., C. Cozzarelli, (1992). "Psychosocial Predictors of Adjustment to Abortion." *Journal of Social Issues,* 48:3:121-142.
125. Risk factors 1-11, see Adler, N. (1979). "Abortion: A Social Psychological Perspective" *Journal of Social Issues* 35:1:109-111.
126. Ney, P. & A. Wickett, (1989). Mental Health and Abortion: Review and Analysis. *Psychiatric Journal of the University of Ottawa,* 14:506-515.
127. Turell, S., M. Armsworth & J. Gaa, (1990). "Emotional Response to Abortion: A Critical Review of the Literature." *Women & Therapy,* 9:4:49-68.
128. Belsey, E., H. Greer, S. Lal, S. Lewis & R. Beard, (1977). "Predictive Factors in Emotional Response to Abortion." *Social Science & Medicine,* 11:71-82.
129. Osofsky, J. & H. Osofsky, (1972). "The Psychological Reaction of Patients to Legalized Abortion." *American Journal of Orthopsychiatry,* 42:48-60.
130. Zakus, G. & S. Wilday, (1987). "Adolescent Abortion Option." *Social Work in Health Care,* 12:77-91.
131. McDonnell, K. (1984). *Not An Easy Choice.* Ontario: Women's Press.
132. See: Ashton, (1980), *op. cit.*
133. See: Adler, N. et al. (1990). "Psychological Responses After Abortion." *Science,* 248:41-44; Ashton, J. (1980). "The Psychosocial Outcome of Induced Abortion." *British Journal of Obstetrics & Gynecology,* 87:1115-1622; Shusterman, L. (1979). "Predicting the Psychological

Consequences of Abortion." *Social Science and Medicine,* 13: 683-689.
134. Freeman, E. (1980) "Emotional Distress Patterns Among Women Having First or Repeat Abortions." *Obstetrics & Gynecology,* 55:5:630-636
135. Additional risk factors 12-14 identified in Rue, Speckhard, Rogers & Franz, 41.
136. Steinberg, 484.
137. See generally Peterson, Prout & Schwarz (1991) 117.
138. See Rue, V. & A. Speckhard, (1992). "Informed Consent & Abortion: Issues in Medicine & Counseling." *Medicine & Mind,* 1:75-94; and Steinberg, T. (1989). "Abortion Counseling: To Benefit Maternal Health." *American Journal of Law & Medicine,* 15:4:483-517.
139. McGrath, E. et al. (eds.) (1990). *Women & Depression: Risk Factors & Treatment Issues.* Washington, DC: American Psychological Association, 12.
140. Nancyjo Mann in Reardon, D. (1987). *Aborted Women: Silent No More.* Westchester, IL: Crossway, xxiv.
141. Stotland, N. (1992). "The Myth of the Abortion Trauma Syndrome." *Journal of the American Medical Association,* 268:15:2078-2079.

# 4

## The Negative Impact of Abortion on Women and Families

*E. Joanne Angelo, M.D.*

Every woman who undergoes an abortion suffers a death experience—the death of her child. This is true even if those around her try to shield her from the reality of her child's prenatal life and the grim details of the abortion procedure. Certain reactions and emotions typically occur in a woman who has undergone an abortion. Although she may temporarily delude herself that the abortion simply removed "a blob of tissue," "a product of conception," or a "pre-embryo," a woman knows her expected date of delivery when, had she not procured the abortion, she would have held a child in her arms. Often, prior to procuring the abortion, a woman begins a relationship with her child, even speaking to him or her by name in her mind, asking the child's forgiveness for what she is about to do.

Other women who have undergone an abortion come to understand the reality of their preborn child's life and death much later—perhaps several years later—and only then begin to deal consciously with their loss and their grief.

Grief is a natural consequence of death—even prenatal death. Current medical and psychiatric literature abounds with articles about grief following perinatal death—death due to miscarriage, ectopic pregnancy, premature death, stillbirth, and Sudden Infant Death Syndrome. E.A. Beer reported, "I can state most assuredly that couples with recurrent, unexplained or explained early pregnancy losses grieve as intensely as those with later losses or losses of liveborn children. Their grief is not visible, however, since society, family, friends, press or clergy do not support or are not trained to support them. Their grief is very real and if unattended can eventually be felt by them to be aberrant, unnatural, or even unhealthy."[1]

Teams of physicians, nurses, social workers and clergy have been developed in hospital obstetrical units to help parents cope with perinatal loss. N.C. Wathen reported, "Ways of helping parents cope with their losses have been recommended and have reduced the frequency of prolonged emotional disturbance and of abnormal grief reaction. . . . These include seeing and holding the dead baby, giving it a name and taking photographs; all help to make the situation a reality and create memories. It is difficult to grieve when no memory of an individual exists."[2]

In his 1990 book, *When a Baby Dies: Psychotherapy for Pregnancy and Newborn Loss,* Irving Leon, a psychoanalyst, explains that "the difficulty in resolving early pregnancy loss such as miscarriage and ectopic pregnancy may be compounded when there is no body to identify, no child to name, nothing concrete to mourn."[3] Like many others, Leon dismisses losses due to elective abortion from the category of losses which must be mourned with the mistaken notion that, since the mother chose to abort her child, she did not have, nor would she later become aware of positive feelings toward her baby.

In 25 years of psychiatric practice, I have been told by a great many women how they agonized over their decision to undergo an abortion—a decision made hurriedly, under duress, and often in a clandestine manner. A woman with an untimely pregnancy often sees no alternative for herself other than abortion and finds no one to help her seek another solution. Confused by her ambivalent feelings about the pregnancy and the pressures which led to her rapid decision to seek its termination, a woman may be surprised by waves of sadness which overcome her along with feelings of guilt and anger after the abortion, especially as the expected date of delivery approaches. Society offers her no support in her grieving. The general expectation is that she will feel relieved that "her problem is solved" and she will be able to "get on with her life" as though nothing significant had happened.

The following quote from Raphael's 1983 book, *The Anatomy of Bereavement,*[4] summarizes my own clinical findings in psychotherapy with post-abortion women:

> For many women, there will be grief to follow and often an undue burden of guilt as well. It is particularly difficult for the woman that she seeks on the one hand to be rid of the pregnancy, yet at the same time mourn its loss. Often, she is expected to feel grateful that she had been able to achieve the termination, as

well she may. Those to whom she might turn for support give her a covert message that her affects should be of pleasure and relief rather than sadness, failing to recognize that the two may coexist. The woman may have required a high level of defensive denial of her tender feelings for the baby to allow her to make the decision for termination. This denial often carries her through the procedure and the hours afterward, so that she seems cheerful, accepting, but unwilling to talk at the time when supportive counseling may be offered by the clinic. (238)

Denial or repression of emotional responses may continue for weeks, months, or years, especially in her contacts with health care providers associated with her abortion experience. (This may seriously color follow-up studies by abortion providers.) Unresolved grief may persist, however, and manifest itself in a number of psychiatric sequelae such as depression, anniversary reactions, post-traumatic stress disorder, psychosomatic symptoms, substance abuse, eating disorders, suicidal tendencies, and dysfunctional interpersonal and family relationships.

In the hours and days immediately following an abortion, pain and bleeding remind the woman of the physical assault on her body, and sudden endocrine changes may cause her to become emotionally labile. Yet societal expectations are that she should conduct herself as if nothing had happened. Her attempts to comply with these expectations may be at great personal expense. She may dose herself with alcohol and sleeping pills to deal with insomnia, nightmares and overwhelming feelings of grief and guilt. She may throw herself into intense activity, work, study or recreation; she may attempt to deal with her feelings of loneliness and emptiness by binge eating alternating with purging or anorexia, or intense efforts to repair intimate relationships or develop new ones inappropriately. All along she may berate herself for not "feeling fine," which she believes is expected of her. Complaints of vague abdominal pain or painful sexual intercourse may cause her to seek treatment from one physician after another unsuccessfully. The very examinations and invasive procedures to which she is subjected may cause flashbacks to the abortion procedure, causing extreme anxiety and great difficulty for her and for her physicians.

A woman who has chosen to terminate a pregnancy may find herself alone to cope not only with the loss of her child who she will never know, but also with her personal responsibility for her child's death. Many post-abortion women report that they are haunted by the intrusive thoughts "I killed my baby! I don't deserve to live!" For them, guilt is not merely subjective or neurotic, it is objective and real.

Reminders threaten their defensive denial and repression all too frequently: the expected birth date of the child and its anniversaries, the anniversary of the abortion, a visit to the gynecologist or gastroenterologist, the sound of the suction machine at the dentist's office or the sound of the vacuum cleaner at home, a baby in a television ad, a new pregnancy, a death in the family, a film depicting prenatal development or abortion. Any of these may trigger a sudden flood of overwhelming feelings of grief, guilt, anger and even despair—which call forth even more intense defensive responses. This cycle typically continues for many months or years before appropriate help is found because, until recently, mental health professionals failed to recognize the many faces of post-abortion grief.[5]

## NORMAL GRIEF AND PATHOLOGICAL GRIEF

Grief is the subjective experience which follows the death of a loved one. Psychiatrists agree that the period of mourning after a significant loss normally continues for at least a year after the death, and if "grief work" is not accomplished appropriately, unresolved grief can produce a variety of psychological and psychosomatic symptoms.

Horowitz[6] divides normal grief into four stages: (1) Outcry, when there may be an intense expression of emotion and an immediate turning to others for help and consolation; (2) Denial Phase, during which the bereaved person may avoid reminders of the deceased and focus attention on other things and when an emotional numbness or blunting may occur; (3) Intrusion Phase, during which negative recollections of the deceased become frequent, including bad dreams and daytime preoccupations which may interfere with concentration on other tasks; (4) Working Through, during which the bereaved person begins to experience both positive and negative memories of the deceased, but without the intrusive, disturbing quality which they had previously, and when emotional numbness lessens. The process of working through has reached completion when the bereaved person once again has the emotional energy to invest in new relationships, to work, to create, and to experience positive states of mind. The medical and psychiatric community is coming to understand that parents who have experienced a perinatal loss can be expected to traverse these stages of grief during at least one year following the death and often, much longer.

Pathological grief occurs when the normal stages of grief are intensified, prolonged or delayed in their expression, and when the bereaved person is not able to resume normal functioning because of the development of other psychiatric or psychophysiologic symptoms. Horowitz[6] describes a pathological *Outcry* phase which may be intensified into a panic state when behavior is erratic and self-coherence is lost in a flood of uncontrolled fear and grief. Alternatively, the bereaved person's withdrawal may be exaggerated into a dissociative state or a reactive psychotic state. I have seen both of these reactions in women immediately following an abortion procedure. These extreme immediate reactions are rarely reported and generally self-limited.

When the *Denial Phase* is pathological, the following may occur: "overuse of alcohol or drugs to anesthetize the person to pain. Some persons may seek to jam all channels of consciousness with stimuli, avoiding thinking and feeling about death. To escape feeling dead and unreal, one may engage in frenzied sexual, athletic, work, thrill-seeking, or risk-taking activities" (67). When pathological grief occurs in post-abortion women, they may be referred for psychiatric care because of substance abuse, "burn-out" on the job, self-injurious or hypomanic behavior.

When the *Intrusion Phase* is prolonged, the bereaved person may be troubled by recurring thoughts or images including nightmares and flashback experiences which may interfere with sleep and daytime activities for months and years beyond the time expected for normal grieving. These persons may present symptoms consistent with a diagnosis of Post-traumatic Stress Disorder. The *Diagnostic and Statistical Manual of Mental Disorders* of the American Psychiatric Association (*DSM-III-R*) includes abortion in a list of life events which may produce sufficient stress to produce Post-traumatic Stress Disorder (what some have termed Post-Abortion Syndrome or PAS) 20.

Depressive illness has long been recognized to be the consequence of unresolved grief. Shakespeare's MacBeth says, "Give sorrow words; the grief that does not speak knits up the overwrought heart and bids it break." *DSM-III-R*[7] states that "morbid preoccupations with worthlessness, suicidal ideation, marked functional impairment, or psychomotor retardation, or prolonged duration suggests that bereavement is complicated by a Major Depressive Episode" (222).

Thus, it is clear that a complicated bereavement (pathological grief) may result in a grouping of symptoms "that warrants diagnosis as one of the anxiety of depressive disorders (including Posttraumatic Stress Disorder), an adjustment disorder, reactive psychosis, or a flare up of a preexisting personality disorder," as Horowitz explains.[8]

## GRIEF AFTER ABORTION

Grief after elective abortion is uniquely poignant because it is usually hidden and often undiagnosed. Years may pass before a post-abortion woman seeks help for a variety of symptoms which interfere with her ability to carry out daily functions at work, at school or at home. Often, only the presenting symptoms are treated without an understanding of their underlying cause. A physician would not think of treating a fever with aspirin without investigating whether it was due to pneumonia, meningitis, heat stroke or flu. Post-abortion grief may not be diagnosed for a number of reasons: (1) The woman may not volunteer her abortion history; (2) The physician or therapist may not be aware of the significance of the preceding abortion; (3) Such a long time may have passed since the abortion that its causative importance may be overlooked. For example, a 75-year-old woman in a nursing home was thought to be psychotic because she was heard muttering over and over again: "I killed my baby! I killed my baby!" In fact, she had had an abortion 60 years before and had never dealt with her loss and her guilt; (4) The accumulation of many negative factors such as failed marriages, "burn-out" on the job, alcohol and drug abuse, eating disorders, and cyclical depression may seemingly be sufficient to explain the severe depression which often brings the post-abortion woman to psychiatric care.

If a woman who is attempting to deal with the loss of a child through abortion makes tentative attempts to share her profound grief and guilt with a therapist who does not hear her pain or who dismisses it as being of little importance, the woman's sense of worthlessness and despair may increase, and she may be confirmed in her conviction that no one will ever understand or be able to help her. She may discontinue her medication, cancel appointments, and sink even more deeply into depression and despair. It is my experience that only when the therapist can endure the flood of primitive emotions which the patient needs to pour out over a number of sessions, without rejecting her or asking her to diminish their intensity, can he or she begin to help the post-abortion woman in her work of mourning.

Neither visual images of a child lost to abortion nor memories of the deceased exist as a resource to help her work through her grief. Her guilt is not merely subjective or neurotic, it is objective and real, and that fact must be acknowledged. However, she has often formed a mental image of her child which haunts her day and night—an image of an infant being torn to pieces, sucked down a tube, crying out in pain, or reaching out to her for help. She may have named her baby and have regularly occurring conversations with him or her in her mind, begging forgiveness for what she has done.

The work of therapy involves allowing her to share these horrific images, and her overwhelming feelings of guilt, shame, anger and grief in the context of a supportive personal relationship. Gradually, she can come to accept the reality of what has taken place and her own responsibility in the death of her child. In time, she can begin to develop a mental picture of her child, no longer suffering or crying out to her in pain but at peace and at rest.

Clergy can be extremely helpful in this process in both helping the post-abortion woman seek forgiveness for herself, and in offering prayers or a memorial service for her child as described by McAll and Wilson's article, "Ritual Mourning for Unresolved Grief After Abortion," in the *Southern Medical Journal.*[9]

Some case vignettes may serve to illustrate the negative impact of abortion on women. Cases involving men and children will be included to illustrate the negative impact of abortion on them and on families as well.

The first case is a young woman who had lost two children to abortion as a teenager, and for whom a new loss became overwhelming and precipitated a suicide attempt. This case also illustrates the importance of assisting post-abortion women to meet their spiritual needs.

CASE #1

> A 23-year-old single woman whom I have called "Joyce" was referred to me after a suicide attempt which involved a planned drunk driving accident. Her obsessive thought was, "I want my

babies!" She had had two abortions, at the ages 17 and 18 while in high school. She was the youngest in a large family and still living at home. Her fear was that if she told her parents (who were older and in precarious health) she had become pregnant twice and had abortions, each parent would "drop dead of a heart attack." She suffered alone for six years with her guilt and the longing for her lost children.

When her uncle who was a priest returned from overseas, she planned to tell him her tragic story. Before she could talk to him, he suddenly died of a heart attack. Mourning his death and now convinced that she would never be able to share her guilt and grief without risking further losses, she planned her own death both to end her pain and to achieve reunion with her children and her uncle, the one priest in whom she dared confide.

The second case is a completed suicide of a young man whose child had been lost to abortion against his will. In this case, a second major loss of a close family member was the immediate precipitant of the suicide.

CASE #2

An 18-year-old gas station attendant, "Peter," shot himself and died three months after his father's unexpected death. Only his closest friend knew that at the time of his suicide, he was despondent over his girlfriend's abortion of their child who, Peter believed, had been conceived on the day of his father's death. In Peter's mind, a mental image of the child had formed. He had told his friend that he would have a son and that he planned to name the boy after his father. The loss of that child and all that he represented to Peter was more than he could bear.

The third case is a 40-year-old divorced woman who sought out a priest first and then was referred to psychiatric care.

CASE #3

"Rhoda" was at the back of the church at a Saturday evening Mass, sobbing uncontrollably, and remained there after everyone had left. Rhoda had wandered into the church in a despondent state because of the sudden breakup of a 12-year relationship with a younger man, although she had not been to church since her abortion more than 20 years previously—which had nearly cost her life.

When the priest returned to the church a half hour later, she begged him to hear her confession. She received the Sacrament of Reconciliation that evening, and attended Mass and received Holy Communion the next day. Because of the multiple traumas in her life and her unresolved grief, she was referred for psychotherapy while she continued to see the priest regularly to help her rebuild her spiritual life.

The fourth case illustrates a Post-traumatic Stress Disorder which developed soon after an abortion and progressed to suicidal depression.

CASE #4

"Nina," a 22-year-old college student was referred six weeks after an abortion because of acute symptoms of uncontrolled crying, intrusive obsessive thoughts about her abortion, anorexia and substance abuse. During the next six months, she lost weight, angered her partner by refusing to be sexually intimate with him and he became abusive to her. She had trouble sleeping, became increasingly agitated especially early in the morning when she repeatedly experienced flashbacks to the abortion experience. She would then compulsively telephone friends and acquaintances whom she felt could have helped her decide against the abortion and did not. She began using alcohol and marijuana early in the morning to control her excessive anxiety. She twice attempted suicide.

Hospitalized twice, Nina was diagnosed as having both Post-traumatic Stress Disorder (PTSD) and a Major Depressive Episode.

"Burn out" on the job and depression were the reasons for the next case being referred for psychiatric care.

CASE #5

An experienced nurse in a newborn intensive care unit was in danger of losing her job because of multiple days out of work which followed the death of premature infants in her care. Instead of helping parents with their grief which was part of her job, "Barbara" was overwhelmed by her own grief every time one of her tiny patients died and was unable to come to work for several days. Barbara had had three abortions, and each newborn death reawakened her own grief which overwhelmed her. She had seen two previous psychiatrists who had treated her with antidepressants but had failed to help her deal with the source of her depression.

The next case is an unusual anniversary reaction in a college student, which illustrates cross-cultural issues.

CASE #6

"Akiko," a Japanese college student, was referred for presumed Premenstrual Syndrome (PMS) which was, in fact, an acute anniversary reaction to her abortion which recurred monthly. One or two days each month, her dormitory staff reported that she would not come out of her room for meals or for classes and spent the time crying inconsolably—a most unusual experience among Asian students in their experience.

Akiko had had an abortion the day before she left Japan to come to the United States to study early childhood education. Her first college classes focused on prenatal development. During a film showing intrauterine life, she suddenly became aware of the actual developmental stage of the fetus she had aborted a few weeks before. From then on, each month on the anniversary of her abortion, she became inconsolable, overwhelmed by sadness and guilt which she could not share with anyone.

In the context of my work with this patient, I learned how women in Japan deal with post-abortion grief. (What I learned from her was also reported in an article in the *Wall Street Journal*.)[10] She explained to me that mothers in Japan often request memorial services for children whom they have lost through abortion. At Buddhist temples, parents rent stone statues of children for a year during which time prayers are offered for babies to the god Jizu. More recently, the goddess Mizuko Kanon is believed to be better able to care for these "water babies," with their smashed heads and shredded bodies because she has large hands with webbed fingers. Parents regularly visit these statues and leave toys, flowers, and written messages for their babies.

In addition to the psychophysiological anniversary reactions described above, the chronic stress of unresolved post-abortion grief can also produce classical psychosomatic reactions as the following case illustrates. The disruption which abortion causes in families is clearly illustrated.

CASE #7

"Jerry" doubled over in pain before a scheduled media appearance. He had not had time for breakfast and had forgotten the antacid medication he regularly took to control the peptic ulcer he had recently developed. Jerry's wife had aborted their first child without his knowledge, and had aborted their second child without his consent. After the birth of their third child, Jerry had become overprotective of the boy, spending every waking moment with him, even changing his work schedule so as to be alone with him while his wife worked. A divorce ensued and sole custody of the child was awarded to his ex-wife. Jerry's grief became profound and his psychosomatic symptoms increased.

Post abortion grief may be responsible for marital conflicts, problems with sexual intimacy, and difficulties in parent-child relationships. Two additional case vignettes will further illustrate these issues.

### CASE #8

"John" was a 28-year-old office worker who entered psychotherapy because of a depressed mood, difficulty sleeping, lack of concentration at work, and conflicts with his wife and children. After several apparently unproductive sessions with his therapist, he reported a dream during which a former girlfriend brought him into a room and introduced him to a ten-year-old boy, and said "This is your son!" Only then did he recall her pregnancy with their child and his active participation in her abortion. Subsequent work with him revealed that his unresolved grief and guilt over that child's death was responsible for his current symptoms.

### CASE #9

"Jeannie" was a six-year-old girl who was referred for evaluation of school-phobic symptoms. Her separation anxiety began at kindergarten and had not abated in the first grade. She often stayed home complaining of stomach aches and headaches. She would only go to school accompanied by her mother; and each time her mother was encouraged to leave, Jeannie would break into terrible screaming and kicking. Jeannie's mother was afraid to leave her in that state even though the teachers assured her that within a few minutes after her departure, Jeannie typically was able to enter the classroom and participate with the other children.

Jeannie's mother had aborted her previous pregnancy—a decision which she deeply regretted. Jeannie was burdened with her mother's pathologically intense attachment to her which did not allow for age-appropriate separation and growth for the child.

The "culture of death" in which we are immersed takes its toll on others beside women who undergo abortion, their partners, and their families.

A recent article in *American Medical News*[11] highlights issues expressed by the women and men who work in the facilities which provide abortions. The National Abortion Federation sponsors workshops for abortion providers where, "they wonder if the fetus feels pain. They talk about the soul and where it goes. And about their dreams, in which aborted fetuses stare at them with ancient eyes and perfectly shaped hands and feet, asking, 'Why? Why did you do this to me?'" (3).

> A New Mexico physician said he was sometimes surprised by the anger a late-term abortion can arouse in him. On the one hand, the physician said, he is angry at the woman. "But paradoxically," he added, "I have angry feelings at myself for feeling good about grasping the calavaria [the skull], for feeling good about doing a technically good procedure which destroys a fetus, kills a baby" (23).

> A nurse who worked in an abortion clinic for less than a year said her troubling moments came not in the procedure room but afterwards. "Many times," she said, "women who had just had abortions would lie in the recovery room and cry, 'I've just killed my baby! I've just killed my baby!' I don't know what to say to these women. . . . Part of me thinks, 'Maybe they're right' " (25).

As more and more of these abortion providers come to a realization of the true nature of their gruesome work, they too will require psychiatric and spiritual care to keep them from despair and self-destruction.

We, the caregivers who reach out to help women and men and their families who have suffered the tragedy of abortion, are affected too by the enormity of the destruction abortion brings about for unborn children and in the lives of those who survive them. We too can become overburdened and lose perspective. The overwhelming needs of those we try to help may be more than one person or one helping discipline can or should try to meet. A team approach is often best. Ideally, these teams include mental health professionals, members of the clergy, volunteers, and, at times, peers who have lived through similar experiences.

Rosters of available psychiatrists, psychologists, social workers, priests, clergy of other faiths, and volunteers can be drawn up and selected names made available to those who seek our help, while protecting the anonymity and confidentiality of the persons in need of care. This multifaceted approach to assisting persons in need assures that the psychological, spiritual and social issues they present will be addressed, and that they will not feel abandoned if one or another caregiver is unavailable from time to time. The team members can educate and support one another in this wonderful work. Team members also need balance in their own lives, time for rest, recreation and prayer, and the availability of personal, professional and spiritual consultation.

## CONCLUSION

The negative impact of abortion in our society is just beginning to be recognized. Thirty million abortions have been performed in this country in the past 20 years and 1.6 million continue to occur each year. This paper has attempted to describe the toll abortion takes on women, their partners, their families, and also on abortion providers and those of us who try to help all of them.

Abortion is one of the "personal tragedies" which the Holy Father spoke of in Denver last month [August 1993] "which must be met with concrete interpersonal acts of love and solidarity." Let us pray that our acts of love and solidarity in the wake of the tragedy of abortion will help to transform this "culture of death" into the "civilization of love" intended by our Creator.

Medical wisdom states that the best treatment for any disease is prevention. Prevention of abortion may come about through offering compassionate alternatives such as support in childbearing, child rearing, and adoption. Ultimately, however, prevention of abortion requires teaching each new generation the true meaning of and reverence for human sexuality, and the dignity of every human person.

## NOTES

1. Beer, EA: "New horizons in the diagnosis, evaluation and therapy of recurrent spontaneous abortion." *Clinics in Obstetrics and Gynecology 1986*; 13:115-116.
2. Wathen, NC: "Perinatal bereavement." *British Journal of Obstetrics and Gynecology* 1990; 97:759-760.
3. Leon, IG: *When A Baby Dies: Psychotherapy for Pregnancy and Newborn Loss.* New Haven, Yale Univ. Press, 1990.
4. Rafael, B: *The Anatomy of Bereavement.* New York, Basic Books, 1983; 238.
5. Angelo, EJ: "Psychiatric sequelae of abortion: the many faces of post-abortion grief." *Linacre Quarterly,* 1992: col. 59, 2:69-80.

6. Horowitz, MJ: *Introduction to Psychodynamics: A New Synthesis*, New York, Basic Books, 1988.

7. *American Psychiatric Association: Diagnostic and Statistical Manual of Mental Disorders*, 3rd ed. rev., Wash., D.C., APA Press 1987.

8. Horowitz, MJ: *Stress-response syndromes: post-traumatic and adjustment disorders in psychiatry*, Michels, et al., eds. vol. 1; ch. 41, Philadelphia, J.B. Lipincott Co., 1990, 8.

9. McAll, K. and P. Wilson. "Ritual mourning for unresolved grief after Abortion." *Southern Medical Journal*, vol. 80, July, 1987

10. *Wall Street Journal*, Jan. 6, 1983, 1.

11. *American Medical News*, July 12, 1993, 3.

12. John Paul II: Prayer Vigil at Cherry Creek State Park, August 14, 1993, Denver, Colorado; "John Paul II Speaks to Youth at World Youth Day. San Francisco: Ignatius Press, 1993, 124.

# 5

# Confronting the Contemporary Medical Contradictions: To Nurture or to Destroy the Preborn Child

*Thomas W. Hilgers, M.D.*

---

## INTRODUCTION

There is a great cultural divide in American society which can also be considered to be, at its core, a great division in values. This is portrayed most poignantly by the recent nomination and probable appointment of Dr. Jocelyn Elders to the position of Surgeon General of the United States.

Dr. Elders has clearly made legalized abortion one of her most important priorities. Indeed, abortion has become the litmus test of the new cultural or value divide. Judges are tested for their favor toward abortion. No feminist group will tolerate a pro-life person as one of its members. The Democratic Party of the 1980's and 1990's stands for abortion in its official platform and its nominees to high political and judicial office. Homosexual groups are strident for abortion. The American Bar Association holds the political position as foundational.

Abortion has become the fountainhead of the divisional stream which was made possible by contraception and has expanded to logically include extramarital sexual activity, homosexuality and euthanasia. All of these forms of sexual activity (plus the right to free "sex" education, condoms and clinics) are considered natural and normal by one side of the cultural and values divide. While these individuals would declare themselves "pro-choice," that is not the value they hold most highly for they are selective in the choices they favor. For example, they are not pro-choice when it comes to many other issues.

The greatest enemy of this American (and Western) cultural movement is the Catholic Church and that is at least one reason why it is so politically correct to ridicule and stigmatize Her. One of the tragedies is that this is done without shame or fear of meaningful reprisal. Indeed, Dr. Elders has verbally abused the Catholic Church in many of her statements.

Unfortunately, the Catholic Church through many of its educational institutions has contributed rather significantly to the very cause of the division of values we observe around us. If it were not for official pronouncements from the highest levels of the Church—including the magisterium—the Church actually would have been quite silent on many of these critical issues. Catholic colleges and universities, hospitals, health care facilities and medical schools, law schools and postgraduate schools have been silent—although insidiously silent—as they have contributed to the abyss of values.

## BACKGROUND

My medical practice is in obstetrics, gynecology and reproductive medicine with a special emphasis on infertility, reproductive disorders, natural family planning and research. Within that context, I see the aftermath of abortion on a regular and routine basis. It is not difficult to see the tears and the regret pour forth with ease when the issue is gently raised and discussed. One has to be blind—and that is one of our problems—not to be able to see these difficulties. Obstetrics and gynecology have become the center of the current storm of medical contradiction—the nature of which clearly illustrates the cultural and values divide.

I have served on the full-time faculty in the department of obstetrics and gynecology at two of the five Catholic medical schools in the United States—St. Louis University School of Medicine and Creighton University School of Medicine. Thus, I have seen directly the impact—or should I say the lack of impact—of Catholic education on the contemporary medical contradictions. In having written extensively on the abortion issue over the last 22 years, I have been promoting alternatives to abortion and have worked side by side with all of the contradictions. In our work in research and application of natural methods of family planning, I have come to recognize that we are noticeably a part of the contradictions—*the other side of the divide.*

## THE MEDICAL CONTRADICTIONS

Planned Parenthood reflects the medical contradictions by saying that every pregnancy should be planned. They do so without any idea of what the word planning means. But quickly, a pregnancy that is *unplanned* becomes a pregnancy that is *unwanted* and out of this comes the clarion and strident call of "Every child a wanted child!" We are now willing to provide abortion to women to whom we previously would have provided *care*ful prenatal care and delivery.

We have become preoccupied with the defective fetus and the *guarantee* of fetal normality. Such a guarantee has led to abortion of the defective child with no scientific or detectable decrease in the number of babies born with fetal defects. That is to say, the killing of the fetus has led to no discernible improvement in fetal health.

We enlist search and destroy techniques to find the child with Downs Syndrome while quite properly promoting television programs which feature a child with Downs Syndrome as one of its adult actors.

We have found that a considerable amount of research has been done over many years on a variety of different issues related to reproductive health, and yet this research tends to be monolithic and the same people who are reviewing the papers for publication are denying the research that is being conducted by people on the other side of the divide. The same can be said for funding applications. This comes not because the scientific standards or methodologies are in error but because of a preconceived prejudice against the philosophical approach.

We have cultivated a profession in which AIDS and other sexually transmitted diseases can be comfortably discussed within the context of their biological causes and their mechanical prevention systems while at the same time exhibiting a total fear and inability—deeply rooted in our retarded emotions as a profession—of being able to discuss and promote abstinence as a solution. In days gone by, we would search out the multiple contacts of a woman who was found to have syphilis so that those contacts could be identified and treated. This was a program which was designed for good public health and to try to curtail the spread of this disease. However, to even consider such a public health program in the current context would be so politically incorrect as to generate vigorous rejection.

With the advancement of abortion has come an increased role for fetal experimentation. With the Clinton administration's recent removal of restrictions on fetal experimentation, this is bound to be expanded. At the same time, surgery is being performed for life threatening illnesses of the fetus while the fetus is still *in utero*—the latter being performed ostensibly for the survival of the fetus to full-term and subsequent health.

We have developed an attitude within obstetrics that obstetrical anesthesia is more important than preparing and educating women for childbirth and bottle feeding is more important than breast feeding. Out of this comes a lack of appropriate education about how the body works and functions and an internalization of the beauty of the human body and, of course, keeping women in true ignorance.

Natural family planning, too, is an educational approach to the achievement or avoidance of pregnancy. And yet, contraception—which is purely chemical or mechanical and clearly not educational—has become the norm. For all of the cries of reproductive freedom, the very system that will allow married couples the freedom of their reproductive systems—through education—that is natural family planning, is denied to them.

In fact, the specific profession of obstetrics and gynecology has become so *totally monolithic* in its attitude with regard to the practice of contraception that young Catholic physicians are being kept out of postgraduate training programs in obstetrics and gynecology because of their attitudes on contraception. This happens in two ways. One way is simply to make it so difficult for the young physician—if they wish not to prescribe contraceptives or sterilization—that they cannot tolerate the pressure placed upon them and they leave the profession. The second way in which this is accomplished is for the young physician to self-select themselves out of obstetrics and gynecology because of the fear that they will have to become involved in practices that they consider to be immoral. In my current position, I have had the opportunity to provide counsel to both groups of young physicians. Indeed, the contemporary medical contradictions that are so pervasive in obstetrics and gynecology are creating, unfortunately, an environment where the Catholic obstetrician and gynecologist is on the verge of extinction.

With the recent calculated move toward assisted suicide, led by Dr. Jack Kevorkian, the drive toward legalized euthanasia is well underway in American society. This is an extension of the contraception-abortion mentality where life is "guaranteed" to be healthy, happy and free of any pain. That lies in contradiction to the caring for the living dignity of our population to the time of each individual's natural death.

WHY IS THIS HAPPENING?

One might ask, why is this happening? Why is it that it has become easier to destroy human life than to nurture it? As one might imagine, with a complex issue such as this there are bound to be many aspects that contribute to this.

In my own reflections on these problems, I have felt for a long time that at the core of these fundamental issues is a *retarded view of our human sexuality*. We live in a society which is stimulated by its hypererotic compulsion toward a *genitocentric* view of human sexuality. Indeed, when one views human sexuality from only the genital perspective, one views the human person as only an organ or a part. There is no substance to the relationship when one views human sexuality from the purely genital perspective.

It is critically necessary that a *totapersonacentric* view of human sexuality be developed. This view would take into account the total person and their spiritual, physical, intellectual, creative/communicative and emotional and psychological components. That is, one would see one's sexuality as a total of one's very being and that true sexual interaction is *mostly* nongenital. In this view, both marriage *and* celibacy derive a richer, deeper meaning.

It is *critically important* that we rapidly move away from the *genitocentric* view of sexuality and move as quickly as possible to a *totapersonacentric* view of sexuality so that our sexuality can be placed into its proper balance. For this to occur, *natural family planning must be accepted* on a widespread basis since it is only natural family planning which allows the married couple to understand their sexuality within the context of this *balanced sexual view*.

Our desires for a painless society have led to the development of a medical profession which is more interested in taking care of what is comfortable than they are dealing with those things that are uncomfortable. While the obstetrician-gynecologist should be interested in the care of women, their actions with regard to contraception, sterilization and abortion show more of a disdain for women than anything else. The physician's unwillingness or inability to deal with what is uncomfortable tends to promote those solutions which are perceived to be "painless." Such approaches as contraception, sterilization and abortion would be considered to be such painless approaches even though there is good evidence to suggest that they are anything but pain-free.

Nonetheless, this emotional immaturity which exists within the personalities of many physicians (and much of society in general) leads to a co-dependency in American society and subsequently in medical practice where the contemporary medical contradictions are accepted and promoted. In fact, it seems to me that we are living almost in a medical culture which has turned so far on its heels as to think that black is now white and white is now black. By that I mean, contraception—be it chemical or mechanical—is now considered "good health." Identifying a fetal defect with its subsequent abortion is considered to be good medical practice. The care of women has developed within the context of an unwillingness to educate them about how their bodies work and function. It can no longer be believed that the unwanted child can ever become a wanted child. The uncomfortable does not exist because everything needs to be comfortable. There is no room for imperfection since the physician guarantees perfection through all of their medical tests and approaches. Within that context, incidentally, we have also generated an extraordinary legal climate where malpractice is epidemic because of claims of imperfection. Post-abortion Stress Syndrome is completely missed because the physician has become desensitized to the very real pain—sometimes rather subtle—that these women suffer.

## THE CATHOLIC CONTRIBUTION

Early on in this discussion, I indicated that in an odd sort of way Catholic institutions have contributed to the development and flourishing of the contemporary medical contradictions. There has been, in my opinion, a distinct failure of Catholic education ever since the mid-1960's when Vatican II seemed to give the impression to many individuals in higher education that the Church was merging its truly Catholic theology into "The Christian Religion" as a generic form of religious expression and thought. In addition, the significant and overwhelming dissent that came like a thunderbolt following the issuance of *Humanae Vitae* created a stigma to the very reality of being Catholic and particularly being a Catholic professor in a Catholic institution of higher learning. This created an environment where the faith was clearly watered down in order to satisfy the perception that this would make it "more palatable."

We have lost two generations of physicians and we are in the process of losing a third generation to the dissent over *Humanae Vitae*. It is no wonder that these medical contradictions are so widespread. There has been so little opposition. This loss of physicians to the cultural divide is a tragedy that must be turned around for us to become successful at ultimately combating these incredible ethical opposites. Indeed, *we need radical change* in the way we educate our young Catholics—in grade school, high school, college and postgraduate school (including medical and law schools). Of the five Catholic medical schools in the United States, *all* provide contraceptives and do sterilizations. At least some of them are involved periodically in the referral for abortion although I don't know of any that are overtly doing abortions.

Nonetheless, the time has come for these medical schools to be called to accountability and change their medical practices dramatically toward natural methods of family planning which are consistent with Church teaching and to teach the young medical students exactly the reasons why the Church teaches what it does.

It is important that such education be presented within the full context of the faith itself and to express clearly the notion that the Church is not acting as "an authoritarian parent" but rather "*as a loving teacher.*" On many issues that the Church deals with—with regard to faith and morals—it is not necessary for us to reinvent the moral-ethical wheel. The Church, like a *loving* parent, can provide insights that will allow us to gain the confidence to move on to more difficult and challenging problems. We must see the Church as one of *the greatest gifts* that Christ has given to us.

While we do live in a pluralistic society—that is people made up of various religions and points of view—there must be developed within such a society the concept of a *pluralistic morality or ethics* and that such a pluralistic morality or ethic needs *to be kept separate and distinct* from those morals and ethics that could be considered clearly *Catholic.*

For example, the prohibition of abortion should not be viewed as the enforcement of one religious ideology upon the whole of society but rather it should be the moral ethic of the entire society thus becoming a reflection of the pluralistic moral dimension of the society itself. Even within that context, any law with regard to abortion will probably not clearly reflect the Catholic moral position (it did not historically reflect that position and there is no reason to think it will in the future).

Our young medical students and undergraduate students need to know the distinctions between *pluralistic morality* and *Catholic morality*. For example, how are they arrived at and upon what authority are they arrived at? Is there a difference between the *politics of compromise* and the *prayer for truth*?

While a *pluralistic morality* is important so that people can *live cooperatively together within a social structure, Catholic morality* is for those individuals who are *searching for the Kingdom of Heaven*. There is a significant difference between a cooperative living arrangement on this earth and the search for truth which leads to the Kingdom of Heaven.

Many of our institutions of Catholic higher education have divorced themselves from true Catholic moral theology and ethics. In so doing, we have been *shortchanging our young people* and subsequently shortchanging the very value basis upon which our Catholic professionals have been recently formed. Indeed, our Catholic institutions are teaching pluralistic morality as if it were Catholic morality, allowing one to consider him or herself a Catholic while not even understanding what that means. One can point specifically to this *defect in Catholic education* as a *cause and effect relationship* to the contradiction that exists.

This radical change that I am discussing represents the *confrontation part* of the medical contradictions—a confrontation which would ultimately move beyond the contradictions and toward the nurturing of not only the preborn child but all of human life. It would deal with the woman who is pregnant and distressed in a way which would eliminate the "need" for abortion. There would be no post-abortion aftermath because there would be no abortion.

The recent papal visit to Denver for World Youth Day clearly exhibits that *young people are searching, yearning and asking for a vacuum to be filled. They* are looking for the truth for they know that the truth will set them free! Indeed, at our recent International *Humanae Vitae* Conference held in Omaha and sponsored by the Pope Paul VI Institute, we felt the same type of energy and spirit coming from people who were truly searching for truth and, in that context, were of one mind, one heart and one soul.

## HUMBLE SUGGESTIONS

I have two suggestions toward the correction of the Catholic educational laxity and the absence of Catholic educational discipline. The bishop of the diocese must take on the responsibility for the Catholic education that is provided in the various Catholic institutions in his diocese (including the colleges, universities and professional schools). I *plead* with those in charge and those in decision making positions to see to it that this be accomplished and that *Catholic educational institutions be called to accountability* on the importance of understanding their role as Catholic educators and propagators of the true Catholic faith. Our young people deserve to be given the opportunity to be properly formed with Catholic faith. Trust in our Catholic educational institutions needs to be reawakened so that parents can properly fulfill their role as primary Catholic educators.

Such a calling to accountability does not need to be harsh or insensitive. I have this suspicion that there are many Catholic institutions that would wish for such leadership from their hierarchy and actually would respond quite favorably to this.

To assist the bishops in this regard, let me suggest that a *pontifical commission* be established with the singular purpose of establishing a *pontifical core curriculum in catholic theology, philosophy and ethics* for use by Catholic undergraduate college and university students for their liberal arts core curriculum. Such a commission could establish a basic core in scriptural studies, the history of the Catholic Church, metaphysics, logic, ethics, the great teachings of the Church, and Catholic spirituality. A university would not be allowed to provide the pontifical core unless they agreed that it be conducted in a way which is fully Catholic and fully in accord with the magisterial teachings of the Catholic Church. By identifying the curriculum as pontifical, this would allow parents the opportunity to decide which college or university to send their children to and it would give them the very specific option of allowing their child the opportunity to grow in the fullness of their Catholic faith. Many parents currently believe this is automatically happening when the young adult child is sent to a Catholic university.

Theological and historical research is necessary for the Church to sustain its intellectual life. In the last 100 years, there have been incredible teachings—in the way of papal encyclicals—that could become the focus of intensive study. Encyclicals such as *Rerum Novarum. Pacem in Terris, Humanae Vitae, Popularum Progressio,*

*Familiaris Consortio, Ex Corde Ecclesiae, Centesimus Annus, Veritatis Splendor,* and many others. Indeed, the *New Universal Catechism* which has recently been released—although not yet in English—is itself a document that should be studied carefully by growing, searching and yearning young Catholics.

## THE NEED FOR SCIENTIFIC RESEARCH

In concluding this, let me also make a significant plea as Pope Paul VI did in *Humanae Vitae* to Catholic scientists—many of whom are represented at this conference today—that they *be given the opportunity* to conduct the scientific research that is so essential and so necessary in this rationalistic world that we live in.

There is nothing fundamentally contradictory in scientific research to the philosophical and theological insights of Catholic teaching. The real challenge, however, is for Catholic scientists to seek out the scientific answers which will allow the world to more pragmatically and objectively see the truths of the Church's teaching.

I believe it to be a responsibility of the hierarchy to see to it that adequate funds are made available—at least some support funds—to see to it that such research is accomplished and carried out.

On a topic such as we are talking about today, "Post-Abortion Aftermath," there has been a significant defect in the pro-life movement in the United States and, for that matter, throughout the Western World. This defect has been in the absence of sound research that is demographic, statistical, psychological, basic science, medical, etc. The absence of an organized research effort has led all of us in this room today to look at each of our efforts as purely individual and barely in connection with anyone else who thinks as we do or sees the world from our eyes.

If we train our young undergraduate students and our young physicians and other postgraduate students in a sound foundational basis for their Catholic decision making, then we shall *unleash before the world a power of truth* that cannot and will not be placed back into the box. You will see these efforts being conducted cooperatively and you will see such institutions as Planned Parenthood, the Alan Guttmacher Institute, the Wayne State Center for the Study of Human Reproduction, etc., all very well funded research institutions, be made scientifically accountable for the first time since the abortion issue has been debated in this country. The only thing that really stands between that accountability and the scientific presentation of the truth is, at the present time, a significant shortcoming in financial support.

## CONCLUSION

I would like to conclude this discussion on a very positive note. In our own work in natural family planning, without going into any great detail, we have developed natural family planning to the point where we can now incorporate it fully within our medical practice. It has become more than just a system of family planning but rather a system of being able to identify reproductive disorders, ovarian cysts, abnormal bleeding; we can better evaluate the woman with Premenstrual Syndrome and subsequently treat her; we can date the beginning of pregnancy from its very beginning, and the list goes on and it will continue to grow as our knowledge grows.

As we have begun to make this change to *NaProTechnology* (the Natural Procreative Technologies), we are beginning to see more and more physicians becoming very excited about natural family planning. There is no doubt in my mind that there are many physicians—and I might point out that many of these are young physicians—who have become very disillusioned living their medical experience in the midst of the contemporary medical contradictions. These young physicians have come to the realization that to nurture is to work within the context of the truth and to destroy is to work in the context of Satan's workshop. Those who have reflected upon it desperately want to be faithful to the Church, to become a nurturing physician and to become a Catholic leader within their communities.

These are exciting times, and the only way in which the contemporary medical contradictions to either nurture or destroy the preborn child or any human person will ever be challenged and stopped is by confronting them with the truth!

# 6

## Emotional and Physical Effects of Pregnancy Loss on the Woman and Her Family: A Multi-centered Study of Post-Abortion Syndrome and Post-abortion Survivor Syndrome

*Philip G. Ney*

---

### INTRODUCTION

Truth has never been accepted in its day. We thank God for a few intrepid investigators and wise communicators—otherwise many uncomfortable facts would never be known. This is particularly true for all those insights which make us most uncomfortable. Truth about the effects of abortion on the family is probably the most discomforting and the least welcome evidence the world must deal with today.

We should not be surprised that the wholesale killing of innocent children has a destructive impact on the individuals directly involved. What has gone mostly unreported is its deleterious consequences for the family. More particularly, humans refuse to recognize what abortion has done to the ecological balances that maintain our species. From our research it is possible to extrapolate into the future and predict that unless these balances be corrected, the species cannot survive.

Every investigator has a bias. It is best that these be stated at the outset. Mine are as follows: (1) There is only one truth; (2) If we do not learn from history we must repeat it; (3) What is bad for the recipient is as bad for the giver. We cannot benefit at the expense of our neighbor. If it is good for him, it is good for us (Universal Ethic of Mutual Benefit); (4) The more uncomfortable the truth to an individual's self-righteous self-perception, the less likely it is to be accepted; (5) The first original sin was to be or to be like

God. The second original sin was to know good and evil. Now it is
. not possible to know one without the other.

## METHODOLOGY

The following findings are based on two major ongoing studies. We are collecting information from a variety of clinical populations of woman in Canada, the United States, Ireland, France and
China regarding the effects of all kinds of pregnancy losses on general emotional and physical health. This data is obtained by self-re-
port on valid and reliable questionnaires. It was collected mostly
from patients who were given the questionnaire while waiting to see
their family physician. Most of the measures are visual analogue
scales, giving us the opportunity to record the full range of effects
on health. To date we have a sample of 3,300 women. The main
sample of women have similar demographic characteristics to the
general population in that age group. Although there are slightly
more married women, we can generalize our findings at least to
North America.

The second study is an assessment of the impact of child abuse
and neglect. Our sample includes a variety of clinical populations of
children, men and women and a contrast group from a normal high
school. Assessments were made independently by the child, the parents, and by a staff member. We have used visual analogue scales to
measure the causes and effects of physical abuse, verbal abuse,
physical neglect, emotional and intellectual neglect, and sexual
abuse.

From our assessments, done in a variety of ways, we believe
we have assessed our questionnaires and established their validity
and reliability. We believe that the sampling is sufficiently representative of Canadians.

## EFFECTS OF PREGNANCY LOSS ON WOMEN'S HEALTH

Table 1 shows the outcome of pregnancies at various ages of
women in Canada on which most of these statistics are based. As in
most of North America, between 25-30% of teenagers abort their
first pregnancy. It also indicates that when the number of abortions
are subtracted, teenagers are as able as older women to give birth to
full term normal pregnancies.

When a multiple regression analysis is done on the forty-four factors we considered as important to a woman's health, the most important factors are the quality of family life, a loss during the first pregnancy and lack of partner support (Table 2). Table 3 indicates that of all the pregnancy losses, abortion has the greatest impact on a woman's assessment of her present health. These pregnancy losses have a cumulative effect (Figure 1). It appears that the outcome of the first pregnancy is most important in determining the outcomes of the following pregnancies (Table 4). Twenty-one percent of second pregnancies are aborted if the first one is aborted compared to five percent if the first is full-term normal birth weight.

When asked about the direct effects of pregnancy losses on their health, women indicate that abortion and miscarriage have the greatest impact (Table 5). If the other factors are left out of the calculations and abortions are compared to miscarriages, it appears that abortions have approximately twice the impact. If the first pregnancy is aborted, compared to full-term outcome, the miscarriage rate is approximately double in the second pregnancy (Figure 2).

It appears that 22% of the women freely admit they have a moderate to marked need for professional help to mourn their pregnancy loss (Table 6).

It appears from this that all types of pregnancy loss have a deleterious effect on a woman's general health, but abortion has a much greater impact. It seems that when a pregnancy loss is not mourned, it results in a depression in the patient. Depression interferes with the immune system, making the woman more vulnerable to both infections and cancers. Abortion creates more psychological turmoil and the loss is much more difficult to mourn because (1) it creates more complicated conflicts; (2) of the ambivalent regard (love and hate) for the bereaved object; (3) the fetus is never held, named, buried or mourned; (4) there is no one they can talk to easily; (5) it is an event that is not supposed to have happened. Too often physicians not only don't recognize the impact of unmourned pregnancies, but studiously ignore the fact that abortion is an unmourned pregnancy and has a greater negative impact than other losses on a woman's health.


WHY DO WOMEN ABORT?

When the computer does a logistic regression on all the factors we considered that might contribute to why women abort, it appears four factors—lack of partner support, young age, marital status and low objection to abortion—are the most important (Table 7). When all kinds of losses are considered, it appears that these are more likely to occur where there has been a previous loss and where there is not sufficient partner support. The third pregnancy is shown here as an example (Table 8).

PARTNER SUPPORT

Both the miscarriage and the abortion rate is much higher when the partner is not supportive or is absent. In the first pregnancy, the abortion rate is four times greater if the partner is not supportive and six times greater if he is absent (Table 9). In the second pregnancy, the abortion rate is seven times greater if he is not supportive and eighteen times greater if he is absent (Table 10). It appears that the miscarriage rate is double if the partner is not supportive, but not greater if he is absent. The importance of partner support continues till the sixth pregnancy (Table 11), but whether the partner is present at birth or not seems unimportant to the pregnancy outcome. The lack of partner support is more important than the total number of pregnancies and the young age of the women in determining the total of number of abortions (Table 12). Whether a loss of the second pregnancy has a deleterious effect on a woman's health mainly depends on whether the partner is supportive, whether her health was affected by a first pregnancy loss, and whether or not she is young (Table 13). It appears from Tables 14 and 15 that the reason more young women abort is because they have less partner support. It should be remembered that the miscarriage rate is greater if there has been a previous abortion. We also found (Table 15, 16) that the miscarriage rate is greater among those who support a woman's right for abortion. We found that patients of doctors who belong to the Christian Medical and Dental Society are much less likely to have abortions and miscarriages (Table 17).

From these findings, I think it can be safely deduced that one of the most important elements in maintaining a pregnancy is to ensure partner support. It appears that a substitute for the partner support by caring Christian physicians can reduce the incidence of miscarriage and abortion. Although the mechanism is not clear, there may be a neurohormonal as well as psychological component to pregnancy losses. This could explain why the miscarriage rate is also higher when there is insufficient support from the partner.  ·

## DATA FROM OTHER COUNTRIES

It appears that there are differences in European countries and China that have yet to be thoroughly explored. However, in all these countries, the data shows that pregnancy losses of all types, particularly abortions, create major health problems. Our data from China is based on only 400 patients, and so I am not completely confident in the results. However, though these patients enjoy being parents and have more partner support than Canadians, their emotional and physical health is as much affected by pregnancy losses (Figure 3,4).

## CHILD ABUSE AND ABORTION

It appears (Table 18) that women who have had an abortion or a miscarriage are more likely to severely verbally abuse, physically neglect, or emotionally neglect their children. Those who have lost a child by miscarriage or abortion are more likely to sexually abuse their children (Table 19). There are high correlations between the mother's tendency to abuse or neglect her children and her propensity to respond to their crying with sadness, anxiety, helplessness or anger (Table 20). Mothers who neglect their children are more likely not to have breastfed or held their babies at an early age. Children who are neglected are more susceptible and vulnerable to abuse. From a child's point of view, the most important causes of abuse and neglect are marital discord, parental immaturity, and parental alcoholism (Figure 5).

From these and other studies, it seems likely that women who have had an abortion are not as able to bond to their next child. They are more likely to respond with fear and anxiety, and are unable to touch the child as often. Therefore they cannot breastfeed them as well. The fact that partner support is a major contributing factor in both pregnancy losses and child abuse and neglect is added evidence that a family is vital.

## POST-ABORTION SURVIVOR SYNDROME (PASS)

We are now collecting data on people who have experienced various kinds of abortion survivor syndrome. There are ten types, and these are as follows:

1. Children who had a statistically low chance of surviving a pregnancy. Children in some Eastern European countries have approximately a 10% chance of surviving through a pregnancy.
2. Children whose parents carefully considered terminating them in utero.
3. Children who have had a brother or sister or both aborted, either before or after they were born.
4. Children who have been threatened by such statements as, "You wretched, ungrateful child. I have sweated and saved for you but you do nothing with your life. I should have aborted you!"
5. Children who know their chances of being aborted are higher because they are handicapped, are the "wrong" sex or are the result of a mixed marriage. Children with developmental defects often wonder whether their parents would have aborted them if they had known.
6. Those children whose parents would have aborted them if they could have.
7. Children whose parents could not make up their mind and delayed until it was too late for an abortion.
8. Children whose twin was aborted. Twins have an intimate relationship in the womb. If one is aborted, the other feels terrible and is often suicidal.
9. Children who survived deliberate attempt to terminate their lives by saline, suction curettage or hysterotomy. They have difficult psychological struggles, nightmares, confused identities and a fear of doctors.
10. Those tiny children who survived an abortion for a short period of time, but then were left to expire on a cold slab or were smothered by clinic staff.

There are terrible conflicts that arise from these situations, and these have an impact on the individual and on society. Now that there are millions of those who have survived abortion, it is important to measure the effect of abortion on the function of a society. Observations indicate that in countries where there have been high rates of abortion, there is the greatest degree of economic chaos, governmental ineptitude and social unrest.

## CONCLUSION

Abortion has devastating effects on a woman and the aborted infant's siblings. Blessed are all those children who grow up in a home where abortion was not even considered. They are free from all the difficult conflicts experienced by abortion survivors. These blessed children are not alive because they were wanted, but because they have an inherent right to life. Because they do not have to strive to stay wanted, they can be more independent and develop as God intended them to do.

God-fearing physicians, priests, pastors and counsellors should have no fear of recognizing the very unpalatable truth of abortion survivors. We hope that they will bring up the subject with their patients, especially with those patients who have many psychosomatic symptoms for which there does not seem to be any other explanation. When they can broach the subject and explain Post-Abortion Survivor Syndrome to their patients, there is often a sense of great relief. Later on, the patients may require extensive psychotherapy. At least now they know why they have such an ambivalent attitude about life, their own life in particular.

## Table 1
## Effect of Age on Outcome of First Pregnancy

| Pregnancy Outcome | Age At First Pregnancy | | | |
|---|---|---|---|---|
| | 14-19 (25.2%) | 20-25 (45.0%) | 26-30 (22.7%) | 31 and up (7.2%) |
| Full term, normal birth weight | 50.4 | 69.6 | 71.8 | 68.8 |
| Full term, low birth weight | 4.3 | 4.2 | 4.4 | 1.3 |
| Premature | 3.2 | 6.8 | 3.6 | 2.5 |
| Miscarriage | 12.5 | 9.8 | 13.9 | 20.0 |
| Abortion | 26.8 | 8.4 | 4.0 | 5.0 |
| Stillborn | 1.4 | 0.6 | 1.6 | 0.0 |
| Early Infant death | 1.4 | 0.2 | 0.0 | 1.3 |
| Ectopic | 0.0 | 0.4 | 0.8 | 1.3 |
| | 100% | 100% | 100% | 100% |
| Full term, normal birth weight, not aborted | 77.2 | 78.0 | 75.8 | 73.8 |

N = 1112     $x^2$     p<0.0000
Figures expressed as percentages

## Table 2
## "My Present Health Is Affected By"

|  | T | SIG. |
|---|---|---|
| My family life | 4.594 | 0.0000 |
| Previous loss* | 2.838 | 0.0048 |
| Whether partner is supportive | 2.478 | 0.0137 |

*in first pregnancy
Expressed as a multiple regression

## Table 3
## Negative Effect on Mother's Present Health of Number of Pregnancies Ending in Various Outcomes

| Pregnancy Outcome | Pearson Correlation Coefficient | Significance |
|---|---|---|
| Full term, normal birth weight | 0.035 | p= 0.190 |
| Full term, low birth weight | 0.058 | p= 0.030 |
| Premature | 0.013 | p= 0.617 |
| Miscarriage | 0.054 | p= 0.041 |
| Abortion, induced | 0.107 | p <0.000 |
| Stillbirth | 0.022 | p= 0.403 |
| Early Infant Death | 0.029 | p= 0.268 |
| Ectopic | 0.004 | p= 0.895 |

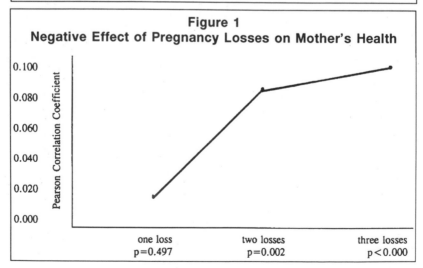

## Figure 1
## Negative Effect of Pregnancy Losses on Mother's Health

| one loss | two losses | three losses |
| p=0.497 | p=0.002 | p<0.000 |

## Table 4a
## The Effect of the First Pregnancy's Outcome
## on the Second's Outcome

| | Outcome of Second Pregnancy | | | |
|---|---|---|---|---|
| *Outcome of First Pregnancy* | Full term, normal birth weight | Full term, low birth weight | Premature | Miscarriage |
| Full term, normal birth weight | 76.9 | 3.5 | 4.0 | 9.3 |
| Full term, low birth weight | 55.9 | 17.6 | 8.8 | 8.8 |
| Premature | 45.2 | 4.8 | 33.3 | 14.3 |
| Miscarriage | 61.0 | 5.9 | 4.2 | 21.2 |
| Abortion, induced | 51.4 | 9.3 | 2.8 | 14.0 |
| Stillborn | 58.3 | — | 25.0 | 16.7 |
| Early infant death | 80.0 | — | — | 20.0 |
| Ectopic | 60.0 | — | 20.0 | 20.0 |
| Figures expressed as percentages | | | | cont'd |

## Table 4b
## The Effect of the First Pregnancy's Outcome
## on the Second's Outcome (cont'd)

| | Outcome of Second Pregnancy | | | |
|---|---|---|---|---|
| *Outcome of First Pregnancy* | Abortion, induced | Stillborn | Early infant death | Ectopic |
| Full term, normal birth weight | 4.6 | 0.4 | 1.1 | 0.4 |
| Full term, low birth weight | 2.9 | 2.9 | 2.9 | — |
| Premature | — | 2.4 | — | — |
| Miscarriage | 5.9 | 1.7 | — | — |
| Abortion, induced | 21.5 | — | 0.9 | — |
| Stillborn | — | — | — | — |
| Early infant death | — | — | — | — |
| Ectopic | 60.0 | — | 20.0 | 20.0 |
| Figures expressed as percentages | | | | |

## Table 5
## My Health Is Negatively Affected
## by Previous Pregnancy Loss

| | # of Full Term, normal birth weight | # of Premature | # of Miscarried | # of Abortions | # of Stillborn | # of Early Infant Deaths |
|---|---|---|---|---|---|---|
| Health negatively affected by previous loss of child or pregnancy | -0.0614 | 0.0139 | 0.2124 | 0.1887 | 0.1435 | 0.0889 |
| | p= 0.045 | p= 0.650 | p<0.0000 | p<0.0000 | p<0.0000 | p<0.004 |

N= 1070
Expressed as Pearson's Correlation Coefficients

## Figure 2
## How the Outcome of the First Pregnancy
## Affects the Miscarriage Rate in the Second Prfgnancy

*Outcome of 1st Pregnancy*          *Miscarriage Rate in 2nd Pregnancy*

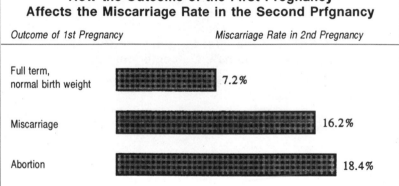

Full term, normal birth weight    7.2%

Miscarriage    16.2%

Abortion    18.4%

## Table 6
## Effect of the Immediacy of a Pregnancy Loss* on the Mother's Need for Professional Help

| Mother's Need | Loss in First Pregnancy | Loss in First And Last Pregnancies | Loss in Last Pregnancy |
|---|---|---|---|
| No need for professional help | 80.9% | 64.9% | 67.4% |
| ↓ | 6.6 | 9.6 | 3.5 |
| ↓ | 1.6 | 8.8 | 5.8 |
| ↓ | 0.5 | 2.6 | 1.2 |
| ↓ | 5.5 | 7.9 | 5.8 |
| ↓ | 2.2 | 0.9 | 5.8 |
| ↓ | 0.5 | 4.4 | 1.2 |
| ↓ | 1.1 | 0.9 | 4.7 |
| Needs a great deal of help | 1.1 | 0.0 | 4.7 |
| | 100% | 100 % | 100% |
| | N = 183 | N = 114 | N = 86 |

Pearson Correlation Coefficient = 0.754. p<0.0000
Chi square = 391.216. p<0.0000
* Losses include miscarriages, stillbirths, and induced abortions

## Table 7
## What Determines Whether a Woman Will Abort Her First Pregnancy? Summary of Logistic Regression

| Factor | Chi-Square | Significance |
|---|---|---|
| Partner not present or supportive | 58.815 | p<0.000 |
| Young age | 21.831 | p<0.000 |
| Not married | 18.349 | p=0.003 |
| Low objection to abortion | 7.125 | p=0.008 |

## Table 8
## Factors Relating to the Outcome of the Third Pregnancy

| *Full Term* | *Loss* |
|---|---|
| 1. Partner generally supportive | 1. Health affected by previous loss |
| 2. Health not affected by previous loss | 2. Partner not supportive during third pregnancy |
| 3. Partner supportive during second pregnancy | 3. Partner not generally supportive |
| 4. Partner supportive during third pregnancy | 4. Partner not supportive during second pregnancy |
| 5. No previous pregnancy losses | 5. Loss of first pregnancy |

Logistic Regression

## Table 9
## Effect of Partner's Presence and Support
## on the Outcome of the First Pregnancy

| | *First Pregnancy* | | |
| | *Present and* | *Present, not* | |
| *Pregnancy Outcome* | *Supportive* | *Supportive* | *Absent* |
|---|---|---|---|
| Full term, normal birth weight | 76.3 | 47.1 | 55.3 |
| Full term, low birth weight | 4.0 | 8.8 | 1.6 |
| Premature | 4.7 | 6.9 | 7.3 |
| Miscarriage | 8.7 | 18.6 | 8.9 |
| Abortion, induced | 4.0 | 16.7 | 25.2 |
| Stillborn | 1.1 | 1.0 | 0.8 |
| Early infant death | 0.8 | 0.0 | 0.0 |
| Ectopic | 0.3 | 1.0 | 0.8 |
| | 100% | 100% | 100% |
| Combined abortion and miscarriage | 12.7 | 35.3 | 34.1 |

N = 969
$X^2$ significance <0.0000

## Table 10
## Effect of Partner's Presence and Support
## on the Outcome of the Second Pregnancy

| | Second Pregnancy | | |
| --- | --- | --- | --- |
| Pregnancy Outcome | Present and Supportive | Present, not Supportive | Absent |
| Full term, normal birth weight | 78.6 | 62.7 | 46.8 |
| Full term, low birth weight | 5.4 | 6.7 | 9.7 |
| Premature | 5.3 | 8.0 | 12.7 |
| Miscarriage | 7.8 | 12.0 | 9.7 |
| Abortion, induced | 1.1 | 8.0 | 19.4 |
| Stillborn | 0.5 | 0.0 | 1.6 |
| Early infant death | 1.0 | 2.7 | 0.0 |
| Ectopic | 0.3 | 0.0 | 0.0 |
| | 100% | 100% | 100% |
| Combined abortion and miscarriage | 8.9 | 20.0 | 29.1 |

N = 764
$X^2$ significance <0.0000

## Table 11
## Significance of Age and Partner Support
## for Pregnancy Outcomes

| Factor Influencing Outcome | Pregnancy Number | | | | | |
| --- | --- | --- | --- | --- | --- | --- |
| | 1st | 2nd | 3rd | 4th | 5th | 6th |
| Age | 116.607 p<0.000 | 78.541 p<0.000 | 32.374 p=0.054 | 19.212 p=0.379 | 20.571 p=0.302 | 9.631 p=0.648 |
| Partner present and supportive | 106.503 p<0.000 | 86.286 p<0.000 | 78.768 p<0.000 | 60.275 p<0.000 | 7.638 p=0.006 | 5.577 p=0.694 |
| Partner at birth | 2.892 p=0.895 | 1.407 p=0.965 | 33.545 p<0.000 | 0.185 p=0.999 | — | — |

Expressed as Chi-Squares

**Table 12**
**Most Important Factors Related**
**to a Higher Number of Abortions**

| Factor | T | SIG T |
|---|---|---|
| Less supportive partner | 7.236 | 0.0000 |
| Higher number of pregnancies | 6.161 | 0.0000 |
| Younger age now | 3.191 | 0.0015 |
| Based on a multiple regression analysis | | |

**Table 13**
**Significant Factors Affecting a Loss**
**in the Second Pregnancy**

| Factor Influencing Outcome | Improvement Chi-Square | p - value |
|---|---|---|
| Partner present and supportive, second pregnancy | 23.686 | 0.000 |
| Health affected by previous loss | 15.671 | 0.000 |
| Age at second pregnancy | 10.206 | 0.001 |
| Summary of stepwise results | | |

**Table 14**
**Frequency of Partner Support by Mother's Age**
**at First Pregnancy**

| | Mother's Age at First Pregnancy | | | |
|---|---|---|---|---|
| | 14 - 19 | 20 - 25 | 26 - 30 | 31 and up |
| Partner present and supportive | 54.5 | 79.9 | 91.0 | 89.0 |
| Partner present, not supportive | 15.2 | 10.3 | 5.3 | 8.2 |
| Partner absent | 30.4 | 9.8 | 3.7 | 2.7 |
| | 100 % | 100 % | 100 % | 100 % |
| | N = 283 | N = 521 | N = 273 | N = 93 |

## Table 15
## Frequency of Partner Support by
## Mother's Age at Second Pregnancy

|  | *Mother's Age at Second Pregnancy* | | | |
|---|---|---|---|---|
|  | *14 - 19* | *20 - 25* | *26 - 30* | *31 and up* |
| Partner present and supportive | 51.5% | 77.9 | 92.8 | 89.3 |
| Partner present, not supportive | 25.8 | 11.2 | 4.9 | 7.4 |
| Partner absent | 22.7 | 10.9 | 2.3 | 3.3 |
|  | 100% N = 82 | 100% N = 380 | 100% N = 308 | 100% N =136 |

## Table 16
## Effect of the Mother's Feeling About Abortion
## on the Miscarriage Rate in the First Pregnancy

|  | *Outcome of First Pregnancy* | |
|---|---|---|
| *My Feeling about Abortion* | Full Term | Miscarriage |
| Approve | 48.1% | 56.2% |
| Sometimes approve | 27.3 | 20.8 |
| Disapprove | 24.6 | 22.9 |
|  | 100 % N = 741 | 100 % N = 151 |

Pearson's R= 0.05372  p= 0.055

# Table 17
## Outcomes of Teenage Pregnancies:
## Victoria and C.M.D.S. Physicians' Patients

| Pregnancy Outcome | Including Abortions | | Not Including Abortions | |
|---|---|---|---|---|
| | Victoria Doctors | C.M.D.S. Doctors | Victoria Doctors | C.M.D.S. Doctors |
| Full term, normal birth weight | 50.4 | 72.0 | 68.9 | 80.6 |
| Full term, low birth weight | 4.3 | 2.5 | 5.9 | 2.8 |
| Premature | 3.2 | 6.6 | 4.4 | 7.4 |
| Miscarriage | 12.5 | 6.2 | 17.1 | 6.9 |
| Abortion | 26.8 | 10.7 | — | — |
| Stillborn | 1.4 | 1.2 | 1.9 | 1.3 |
| Early infant death | 1.4 | 1.2 | 1.9 | 0.4 |
| Ectopic | 0.0 | 0.4 | 0.0 | 0.4 |
| | 100 % N = 280 | 100 % N = 243 | 100 % N = 280 | 100 % N = 243 |

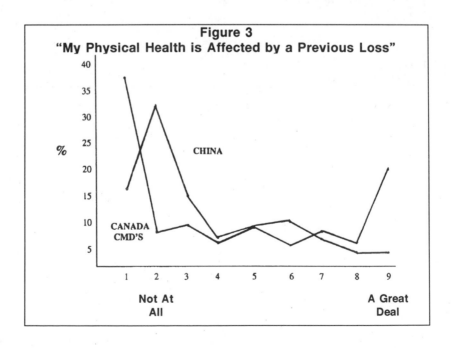

# Figure 3
## "My Physical Health is Affected by a Previous Loss"

CHINA

CANADA
CMD'S

Not At
All

A Great
Deal

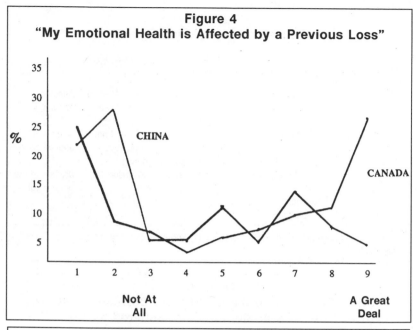

## Figure 4
## "My Emotional Health is Affected by a Previous Loss"

## Table 18
## Correlation Between Mother's Previous Abortion(s) and Her Mistreatment of Her Child

| Type of Mistreatment | Spearman Correlation Coefficient | Significance |
|---|---|---|
| Severe verbal abuse | 0.308 | p= 0.03 |
| Severe physical neglect | 0.308 | p= 0.03 |
| Severe emotional neglect | 0.265 | p= 0.05 |

## Table 19
## Causes of Abuse and Neglect

| Physical Abuse | Verbal Abuse | Physical Neglect | Emotional Neglect | Sexual Abuse |
|---|---|---|---|---|
| Lack of breast-feeding* | Husband not supportive during pregnancy | Husband not home during pregnancy | Breast-feeding not enjoyable | Affected by abortion loss |
| Husband not home during pregnancy | Breast-feeding not enjoyable | Affected by death of spouse or close friend | Husband not supportive during childhood | Number of abortions |
| | Fear of losing pregnancy | | | Breast-feeding not enjoyable |

*length of breast feeding determined mostly by (1) how enjoyable and (2) quality of touch (initial reaction)

## Table 20
## Mother's Response to the Child's Cry Correlated with the Type and Severity of Mistreatment Suffered by the Child

| | Type of Mistreatment | | | |
|---|---|---|---|---|
| Mother's Response | Physical Abuse | Verbal Abuse | Physical Neglect | Emotional Neglect |
| Anxious | 0.028 (22) | .227 (23) | .506 (7) | .168 (10) |
| Angry | .285 (19) | .286 (21) | .079 (4) | .204 (8) |
| Sad | .164 (22) | .057 (22) | .498 (6) | .512 (9) |
| Helpless | .017 (23) | .136 (23) | .545 (6) | .441 (9) |

Expressed as Pearson Correlation Coefficients
Number of cases for each cell in parentheses

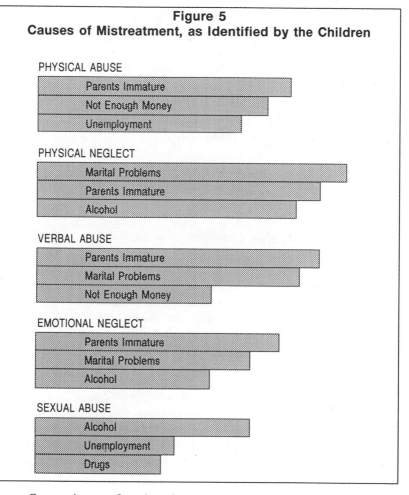

**Figure 5**
**Causes of Mistreatment, as Identified by the Children**

PHYSICAL ABUSE
- Parents Immature
- Not Enough Money
- Unemployment

PHYSICAL NEGLECT
- Marital Problems
- Parents Immature
- Alcohol

VERBAL ABUSE
- Parents Immature
- Marital Problems
- Not Enough Money

EMOTIONAL NEGLECT
- Parents Immature
- Marital Problems
- Alcohol

SEXUAL ABUSE
- Alcohol
- Unemployment
- Drugs

Causes given on Questionnaire:
Alcohol abuse
Drug abuse
Parents immature
Professional interference
Too many children
Not enough money
Grandparent interference
Unemployment
Marital problems

# 7

# The Cultural Impact of Abortion and Its Implications for a Future Society (Part One)

## Jean Garton, Litt.D.

It was a little after midnight on a June summer night a few years ago when a section of Interstate 95 collapsed over the river in Greenwich, Connecticut.

At that moment, a young couple driving to a wedding in Maine was on the bridge behind a trailer truck loaded with meat. The truck suddenly fishtailed, and the young man driving the car jammed on the brakes as he and his wife braced for the inevitable crash. Instead, the truck disappeared into a black hole as the car screeched to a halt just ten feet short of the gaping chasm.

In his rear view mirror, the young man saw the lights of an approaching car. He ran back along the highway divider, yelling and frantically waving his arms, trying to warn the oncoming vehicle. But the car, with two young males, never slowed. Instead, the driver made an obscene hand gesture at the lonely figure desperately trying to warn him. It was his last action before he and his passenger plunged over the edge to their death.

Two people—strangers—had messages for one another. One tried to warn the other of impending tragedy. The other responded with disdain, contempt and suicidal cynicism.

Sound familiar? It will to those who have attempted to warn this society of the disaster the awaits an individual or a culture that tries to solve social, economic or personal problems by eliminating "problem" people.

Yet that tragic event in Connecticut led me to wonder about what might have stopped those young people. Would they have paid attention if, instead of one lonely figure standing there, there had been a whole string of people? A life chain? Or a rally? Or a march? A prayer vigil?

Would they have paid attention if the person issuing the warning, instead of being in jeans and a tee-shirt, had been an authority figure? A state trooper, perhaps? A physician in a white coat? A member of the clergy with a collar?

We will never know for sure what, if anything, might have stopped those young people, but of one thing we can be sure: they were not the only victims of that tragedy. Also victims were their fathers and mothers, brothers and sisters, girlfriends and classmates. Their schools, communities, churches—all were affected in some way.

So, too, in the matter of abortion. What is promoted as a private matter has far-reaching public implications and makes victims of many others. Consider just a few.

## THE MEDICAL PROFESSION AS VICTIM

Abortion has been promoted among physicians as a "treatment" to be added to their arsenal of cures. As a result, we have seen an acceptance of killing in the name of healing.

Yet what happens to a medical profession that engages in killing unborn children—in staggering numbers—not passionately (as in child abuse); not fanatically (as in the Jim Jones massacre in Guyana); not neglectfully (as through starvation in Somalia); but coldly, detachedly and very, very lucratively?

What happens to Western Medicine, the most compassionate, humane medicine in the world, when it reverts to pagan practice in which a doctor becomes both healer and exterminator at the same time?

## WOMEN AS VICTIMS

In abortion, nature becomes the woman's opponent and, as an old commercial said, "You can't fool Mother Nature." A woman can have an ex-lover or an ex-husband but never an ex-child—only a living child or a dead child but a child, nevertheless, written forever on her biological consciousness.

Because abortion—an unnatural act—contradicts a woman's maternal inclinations and instincts to protect her own flesh, it has created a sorority of permanently scarred women. Secular (and often religious) counseling discounts the guilt which many women experience, making her feel guilty about feeling guilty. The issue, of course, isn't "feeling guilty." It is guilt.

These millions of abortion-wounded women are in homes and classrooms today where they are raising tomorrow's children. Given the need of many to justify and defend their actions, what will these women pass on to the next generation in regard to self-control, duty, and accountability, sacrifice?

Women are the repositors of values, and it is the moral fiber of the women of a country that determines the moral fiber of that country. We are always, only one generation away from paganism. How able are weakened, wounded women to do battle against the barbarism of moral relativism that is knocking on society's door?

## MEN AS VICTIMS

Having in theory the God-given right to beget children, no man (married or otherwise) has any legal way to secure that right. Abortion has effectively turned a whole segment of the male population into moral mush, reducing them to the status of the legendary monkeys who are to "see no evil, hear no evil and speak no evil" about "a woman's right to choose."

Yet research indicates that some men are also victims of abortion abuse and suffer grief, anger, and a general sense of impotence about their lives. I received a letter from such a man in which he wrote the following:

> I am at Trenton State Prison as an inmate. I am here having been found guilty of murder. But I have more guilt feelings about an abortion I paid for many years ago than for the crime I am now in prison for. I know God has forgiven I me for that killing, but I have never been able to pray away the guilt feelings I have about my part in the death of an unborn child.

There is something involved in abortion that goes beyond the rhetoric of "a woman's right to choose," . . . beyond our finite scientific understandings of pregnancy and childbirth. Abortion, fundamentally and terrifyingly, as Richard John Neuhaus has said, is about the decline of human significance.

## BORN CHILDREN AS VICTIMS

Women have long sensed that in pregnancy the child they carried was theirs to protect. Abortion, instead, leads women and society to a sense that the child is theirs to possess. The result is a view of unborn children as property—a view that is difficult to revise after a child is born. It is not surprising, then, that abortion has become a significant factor in the escalating epidemic of child abuse.

A special news report in April of 1993 stated that in the U.S. there are four deaths a day from child abuse, with statistics showing a 10 percent increase in 1991. Newsman Dan Rather expressed shock and declared that America has had "a startling rise in child abuse." "Startling" and shocking, certainly, but not surprising given the implications of abortion for the well-being of all children whether born or unborn.

## THE FAMILY AS VICTIM

Abortion can produce a deep, subtle (and often permanent) fracture of the trusting relationship that once existed between a child and parent.

Although children are wonderful observers, they are poor interpreters. Therefore, when children are aware that their mother has had an abortion, some of them struggle with two unspoken questions. The first goes something like this: "If I had been unwanted (handicapped, inconvenient, economically burdensome or whatever reason given by the mother to justify the abortion), would mother have done that to me?"

The second hidden question, logically, is, "If I *become* unwanted (handicapped, inconvenient, economically burdensome, or whatever), will mother do that to me?"

Further, abortion has become, for some parents, the ultimate weapon of discipline. While abortion cannot physically destroy the life of an already-born child, it can destroy his or her quality of life and even his or her will to continue that life.

After I finished a slide presentation on life in the womb, the first hand to be raised with a question was that of a girl of about twelve. "My mother," she announced, "has had two abortions. Why was I allowed to live?"

After the program a woman, who identified herself as the girl's stepmother, expressed her gratitude for my answer and told me that the girl had already attempted to commit suicide twice, wanting to be with her aborted brother and sister.

She explained that in the girl's early years she had lived with her biological mother, and whenever she did something that annoyed or upset the mother, the mother would say, "I wish to hell I'd aborted you, too."

In order to justify abortion we must either discredit children or change them. One way, as Dr. Donald DeMarco has observed, is to see them in terms of deficiencies: what they are not, what they cannot do, and what they do not have. However, in the process, their self-esteem and self-worth (especially of children in their formative years) can be shattered.

With almost thirty million abortions in the U.S. since *Roe v. Wade* in 1973, what impact has abortion had on the psyche of a whole generation of children who escaped their abortion themselves only to find they are secondary victims of the abortion of their unborn brother or sister?


COMMON SENSE AS VICTIM

Some fifty years ago, Louis Evans Sr. said that 75% of all Americans do not think, 15% think they think but only 10% actually do think. (That was before television, so perhaps 10% is high for today.)

Ideological causes tend to lead to the pursuit of ignorance. Once something becomes a cause, common sense seems to evaporate. There is little sense held in common any longer, but there is surely an overabundance of non-sense promulgated under the most socially impeccable auspices.

I was involved in a debate with three pro-choice church professionals, an arrangement, of course, considered "fair" and "balanced" by the sponsoring television staff.

They dominated the discussion with a defense of womens' "rights" and "choices" until, at one point, I asked them to respond to the question, *"When does individual human life begin?"*

The pastor of a congregation said, "We can't talk about individual life—only about a life principle that began back in the Garden. Life is a continuum and cannot be discussed in terms of individuality."

By way of contrast, a television program that same month featured a story about a rapist who had been convicted on the basis of the individuality of his genetic makeup. The host of the show said, "We now have the most reliable test in the world for establishing the *individuality* of each human life. The chance of someone else in the world having the same genetic makeup as you is one in one hundred millionth of one percent or, put another way, one in ten billion chances."

Since the world's population is only five and a half billion, it is obvious that each human life is wonderfully unique, irreplaceable and individual.

The next to answer was a clergyman serving in full-time Christian counseling. He responded by saying that individual human life begins when the mother accords personhood to the child; when she accepts "it" as part of the human family.

Such a subjective view would be laughable if offered in any other context. As a mother who has survived four teenagers, there were times I was quite convinced they were not members of the human family.

If personhood is mine to bestow, ought it not also be mine to withdraw? If "it" is mine to accept at some point, ought "it" not be mine to reject at another point? (The "terrible twos" or the tempestuous teens come to mind.)

Both the law and society rightly reject such a view after birth while accepting its intellectual wrongheadedness before birth.

The third professional in the debate was a Christian ethicist. "Doctor," I asked, "when does individual human life begin?" He responded by tapping his temple a few times and then declaring that individual human life begins in the minds of a man and woman when together they plan to bring a child into the world. Individual human life, he said, begins with their plan to create a new life.

The pastor said, "profound . . . very profound." The counselor said "deep . . . very deep." I said, "Nonsense! Doctor, I have four children, and by your standard the last two had no beginning."

If individual human life does not begin when the male sperm fertilizes the female egg, then the whole concept of biological fatherhood is an arrogant male myth. At no other point—except at that point—does a man contribute anything to the "beingness" of a child.

When Robert Kennedy was assassinated in 1968, his wife, Ethel, was pregnant just a few weeks. Robert was not alive when that child became a fetus at the end of two months. Robert was not alive when that child quickened at four and a half months. Robert was not alive when that child considered viable at six and a half months, and Robert was long dead when that child was born at nine months.

Yet, the Kennedy family, the Catholic Church, the law and society all acknowledged that that was Robert Kennedy's child because Robert was there—at the beginning—when individual human life begins.

## THE CHRISTIAN WITNESS AS VICTIM

Many years ago I had the opportunity to attend a series of lectures by Archbishop Fulton J. Sheen. In one session he proposed that the Christian Church goes in cycles of 500 years and that in each of those cycles there is a major controversy, challenge or test which the Church faces.

In the first five hundred years, said Archbishop Sheen, the challenge was to the *doctrine* of the Church. It centered around the nature and person of Christ, and from that controversy came the great creeds that are still proclaimed today.

The next five hundred year cycle, he said, saw a controversy that centered on the *leadership* of the Church, and that struggle resulted in the Eastern schism.

In the next cycle, said the Archbishop, the challenge was to the *practice* of the Church and culminated in the Reformation.

Now, at the end of another five hundred year cycle, he believed that the test presented to the Church was that of its *witness*. Confronted with the challenge of secularism, he feared we had failed the test.

As a result, he said, we are seeing the end of Christendom—not the end of Christianity—not the end of the Church—but the end of the influence of the Judeo-Christian ethic on the primary institutions of Western civilization.

Two decades later, his words appear more accurate than ever. Christians in every generation are called to forge a counterculture. Instead, many have manufactured a counterpart, living in the aura of Christianity but little of its substance.

For instance, there is the Bible Church that provided the seed money for an abortion clinic. Since there have been abortions throughout human history, said the pastor, obviously, God has "ordained" abortion.

There is the Methodist church leader, speaking of her own abortion of a child conceived through an adulterous affair, who said that together with her two childbirths the abortion was the "holiest" experience of her life.

There is the Lutheran gynecologist who defends doing abortions by saying that children who die from abortion return to heaven and are reborn to another mother.

There is the Episcopalian bishop who, in testimony before a state legislature, said that when a child is unwanted the most loving thing we can do is abort it.

There is the Episcopalian clergywoman who said that abortion should be a sacrament. Indeed, she already knew people who were celebrating it as such.

Such a perverted witness is surely evidence that the human mind is never more clever or resourceful than when it is involved in self-justification. The result, in the words of Aleksandr Solzhenitsyn, is that

> The 20th century has been sucked into the vortex of atheism and self-destruction. . . . The social theories that promised so much have demonstrated their bankruptcy, leaving us at a dead end. (From "Men Have Forgotten God")

Certainly there have been signs along the way that we are heading toward a dead end and toward the degeneration of both American society and Western civilization.

While abortion is but one sign, it is the most disturbing sign, not only because of the monstrous numbers of victims it claims but because it has evolved, in just two decades, from being rejected, to being tolerated, to being accepted, to being celebrated.

The cultural impact of abortion includes "fallout" for a future society in terms of emptying the language of its content, the genocide of minorities, the creation of a top-heavy elderly population, the proliferation of violence and many other ripple effects.

Abortion sets into motion sequential processes that make their way into the ordinary, "nuts and bolts" matters of everyday living. The following are but a few examples.

*LEADERS WITHOUT FOLLOWERS:* Within the body of Christians, there are 20,000 denominations, an overwhelming majority of which have official pro-life policies. Catholics are the largest group, comprising almost half of all Christians. The second largest is the Eastern Orthodox, and the third largest is Lutheran. All three are officially pro-life.

Unfortunately, like abortion, the official views of those church bodies have been seen as a matter of "choice" by some members. That attitude is redefining what it means to be a Roman Catholic, to be a Lutheran, to be a Christian.

Abortion has been a major factor in the diminishing loyalty and faithfulness of members to their denominational teachings. Even more tragic are those members who are pro-life by conviction but pro-choice by apathy. It is terrible for Christians to have convictions without courage (Romans 14:22,23).

*FRONT DOOR LOSSES:* Many churches have begun to develop programs to stem the tide of back-door losses. However, few denominations are giving attention to the impending problem of front door losses—those millions of killed-before-birth children who will impact the viability of parishes nationwide.

By way of illustration, consider the Lutheran Church – Missouri Synod (LCMS) with a religious educational system second only in size to that of the Roman Catholics. More babies are killed by abortion every eleven days in the U.S. than are baptized in an entire year by the 6,000 congregations of that church body.

What are the implications, then, for the parochial school system of the LCMS? For church vocations? For volunteer caring societies and ministries?

If, indeed, we are always only one generation away from paganism, it is obvious that that generation is now sitting in our church pews, at our parochial desks, and around our kitchen tables.

*SOCIO-ECONOMIC SUICIDE:* Having sloganeered the "right" to have abortions into a multimillion dollar industry, the pro-choice people (and all of us) will soon experience an unavoidable economic reality. Fewer growing children, fewer worn out sneakers, fewer diapers used, fewer toys purchased, fewer desks ordered—all mean something economically.

While the missing generation can be calibrated in terms of missing income and missing productivity, there is an intangible that cannot be measured, only mourned. Who will mourn the cures never discovered, the wisdom never taught, the inventions never developed, the champions never honored because of a society that fails to see potential in what it dismisses as "blobs, tissue or products of conception"?

*CHARITABLE CONTRIBUTIONS:* The ascendancy of death solutions for human problems undermines not only morality but humanitarianism as well. The current wave of death-acceptance is reducing the influence of religion, based as it is on the sanctity of life. However, in a human climate in which life itself is cheapened, the influence and viability of every human-care cause is certain to be affected.

Recent studies indicate that charitable giving for humanitarian causes is diminishing because people believe that human problems are too great to be impacted, much less solved. As a result, increasing dollars and grants are going to environmental causes.

What are the implications for the financial support needed to establish and sustain counseling centers and programs for crisis pregnancies and for post-abortion stress?

*SOCIETAL GUILT:* Because abortion has been formalized and bureaucratized, each of us performs a small, and often hidden, part of the national abortion delivery system. It is difficult to see the link between individual action (through taxes, purchases, insurance, etc.) and the final outcome.

Because of these disguises, it is hard to reveal the magnitude of death making in our society. We are all involved somehow, however unwillingly or unwittingly, and we cannot, as a nation, escape the tragic reality of solidarity-in-guilt.

The millions of unseen, unheard, unwanted, unborn human beings who are no more, nevertheless, stand as witnesses against us. History has shown that God will not be mocked. God will have His children but in such a way that they are a judgment on us.

*OTHERS IN JEOPARDY:* Additional groups are at risk of being "made dead." Societies have always set boundaries around themselves and, depending on the prevailing values of that society, have classified various groups of people as nonmembers.

History is replete with examples of this phenomenon: the Supreme Court that excluded Dred Scott from personhood, the Egyptian pharaohs who excluded the Israelites, the Third Reich that excluded the Jews, the Canadians who excluded the Indians, the Australians who excluded the Aborigines.

Times of economic and social stress, however (not unlike the present situation in America), tend to increase the numbers of people seen to be part of devalued groups.

While there is no agreed upon basis for dividing the human family into persons and nonpersons, there is agreement from science that from fertilization we all share a common humanity. We are all members of the "human family," to use the words of the Universal Declaration of Human Rights.

Disenfranchising some members of that family from basic human rights and moral consideration, as is done in abortion, can lead to justifications for marginalizing, oppressing and even eliminating other classes of people.

## CONCLUSION

How precious life must be to God in that it is his first gift to us. Without that first gift, the other gifts of faith, hope and love would have no context in which to exist. Yet life is not only God's first gift to us, it is also his last. If we are faithful, He says, He will give us a crown of life.

Abortion, at its core, is idolatry. It is not just a "Thou shalt not kill" issue, but a First Commandment issue as well. Abortion grounds the identity, security and meaning of human life not in the God who is Creator, Redeemer and Sanctifier, but in self. Abortion sins agains the First Commandment because it fails to receive other human beings as gifts from God.

Abortion constitutes the primary spiritual and moral crucible of this age. Abortion says to the culture that God can't provide and the Church can't help. The culture, in turn, says to the Church that while abortion may not be a good thing, it is usually the lesser of two evils. Why should we offer women an evil of any kind?

After 2,000 years of Church teaching against abortion, it has taken this generation of Christians to find something good in what God has condemned. Frankie Schaefer, Jr. may be close to the truth when he says that over every abortuary in the country there should hang a sign that reads, "This abortion clinic is operating with the permission of your local Christian churches."

Ours is a culture that escapes values by repudiating them. Its lostness is seen in schools that cannot teach, in social work that does not work, in a legal system that itself has become lawless. Such a society is the very negation of society. This culture is in trouble, but this culture is going nowhere unless the Church goes there first.

For those who continue to give witness to the sanctity of life, a quote from the stage production *Another Kind of Hero* is worth remembering. The play, which dramatizes the efforts of Swedish businessman Raoul Wallenberg, who saved the lives of 95,000 Jews during World War II, includes the following line: "Winning is the act of just not giving up."

# 8

## The Cultural Impact of Abortion and Its Implications for a Future Society (Part Two)

*Helen Alvaré*

---

When I assumed my current position, my family's univocal reaction was, "Good, now you can put that nonstop mouth of yours to good use." But even a mouth as legendary in my family as my own could have difficulty covering the breadth of information the above title implies. I have therefore tamed the beast by selecting five of the most significant effects of the widespread practice of legalized abortion. Due to time constraints, there are additional effects which I will list briefly at the end, but not develop at any length.

### ALL TRUTH AS SUBJECTIVE

Whether spoken or unspoken, the presumption underlying support for legal abortion is that there is no objective truth about the value of unborn human life. Before long, that presumption is exported to judgments about all human life. Harvard constitutional scholar Ronald Dworkin exemplifies this development in his new book on abortion, *Life's Dominion*: "[A] state has no business prescribing what people should think about . . . the value of human life . . . and about how that value is respected or dishonored in different circumstances." No distinctions are drawn between any stages of human life.

Every time the word "choice" is substituted for abortion, it is reinforced that the freedom to choose a variety of actions is more important than the objective morality of the action chosen, including the act of choosing *not* to value some human lives. Individual circumstances surrounding a pregnancy become more important than the presence of a human life at the end of the abortion instruments

100

because the circumstances are deemed to subjectively determine the morality of the abortion. Thus the constant use by abortion advocates of worse case, heart-wringing scenarios to justify the need for killing the unborn.

Of course, the violent results of this sort of thinking are evident not only in the 4,400 abortions performed daily, but in a dizzying cycle of violence leaving no segment of *born* humanity untouched either. But abortion advocates refuse to recognize the philosophical and practical ramifications of condoning subjective valuing of human life, nor the social schizophrenia created by telling citizens they must care deeply about the fate of a child a day following birth although they are forbidden to care meaningfully the day before. The result? Neither the born nor the unborn are properly cherished . . . no matter how many bumper stickers display the slogan "pro-child, pro-choice."

SUFFERING AS ABERRATION:

A majority of seemingly different arguments used to justify abortion may really be characterized univocally: abortion prevents suffering. Whether the abortion advocate is claiming that the mother ought to have access to abortion because of her youth, a health problem, rape, poverty, etc., the argument is really the same: if we don't allow abortion, either the child will suffer (e.g. from disability) later, or will cause the mother suffering (e.g. from poverty). Listen to how the U.S. Supreme Court framed the need for legal abortion in the 1973 decision, *Roe v. Wade*:

> The detriment that the state would impose upon the pregnant woman by denying this choice altogether is apparent. . . . Maternity or additional offspring may force upon the women a distressful life and future. Psychological harm may be imminent. Maternity and physical health may be taxed by child care. There is also the distress, for all concerned, associated with the unwanted child, and there is the problem of bringing a child into a family already unable, psychologically and otherwise, to care or it. In other cases, as in this one, the additional difficulties and continuing stigma of unwed motherhood may be involved.

Proponents of this argument usually presume that suffering in the world is an aberration which ought not be part of the human condition. Not only should each of us not be subject to conditions which cause us to suffer, but we ought not to be caused to suffer by another's problems. And even possessing a "quality of life" short of the standard defined by opinion leaders as the "norm" is deemed the equivalent of "suffering." Consider this study released one month ago in France: 42% of French women said that "if they gave birth to a severely deformed baby they would favor killing the child." Ninety percent would abort a child "if made aware of the deformity in the first trimester," 65% in the second and 47% in the third. Forty-two percent said euthanasia of the child would be justifiable if the parents were made aware of a deformity at birth. (*Le Monde*, 8/20/93).

These reactions to suffering take place in a society wedded to believing there are technological solutions to every problem. At the 1993 World Youth Day in Denver, John Paul II reflected:

> In the modern metropolis, life—God's first gift, and the funda-
> mental right of every individual, on which all other rights are
> based—is often treated as just one more commodity to be organ-
> ized, commercialized and manipulated according to convenience.

In the modern mind, convenience includes babies perfect in themselves, and suited perfectly in sex, timing, etc., to the parents' situations. The very availability of surgical and chemical abortion techniques becomes part of the argument to destroy children who may suffer or cause us suffering.

## WOMEN'S GIFT OF FERTILITY AS THREAT

One does not have to travel too far back into history to find commonly expressed the opinion that women's biology, specifically their fertility, is per se problematic, uncontrolled, aberrational. Today, however, we regularly hear this same sexist canard from self-identified "feminists" in the course of their abortion apologetic. And we hear it despite the fact that the modern movement to promote women's dignity and equality was formed, in part, to overcome this sort of thinking.

Every time an abortion advocate claiming feminist credentials proposes abortion as a "solution" to the "problem" of sexism, the message is clear: equality will only be achieved when men and women are in identical situations such that both can engage in sexual intercourse and neither will be pregnant. Women's abilities to become pregnant and to rear children disadvantage women vis-a-vis men and must be 100% regulable by women.

This development drags the legitimate movement for women's dignity back decades. Rather than seeing women's differences as gifts, celebrating them and insisting on social acceptance of them, it singles them out as a "problem" requiring control. In no way will this development dignify women, but rather further reinforce the notion that the male is the norm, women the aberration to be subjugated or changed to "fit" social institutions designed by men for men.

## ATTACKING OFFSPRING AS A MEANS TO SOLVING SOCIAL PROBLEMS

It is a short step from characterizing women's fertility as inherently problematic, to attacking it as an indirect means to solving social problems. The argument usually proceeds as follows: children born ill, poor, unloved, and so on, are the source of tremendous social problems for the children and their mothers; tremendous social resources are consumed in trying to solve these problems, which often, still, go unsolved; legalization of the destruction of unborn life is therefore necessary in order that these children not be born in the first place.

Two phenomena in particular flow from this reasoning. Pro-abortion policies tend to replace policies to directly address the problems driving women in the first instance to the abortion clinics. This is because abortions, at $250 to $1000 each, are seen as a cheaper and quicker "fix" than policies striking at the institutions and structures which pit women and their offspring against each other. Social policies to support women and families, to ensure access to a humane quality of life, to persuade the young to delay intercourse until marriage, to value mothering as a real social contribution, etc., are far more expensive and require a true, deep and lasting commitment to women, children and families.

Empirical data compiled in Mary Ann Glendon's *Abortion and Divorce in Western Law* support this "replacement theory." Numerous examples exist in the United States, including recent legislative proposals to require women to have the five-year contraceptive (Norplant) surgically implanted as a condition for continued receipt of welfare benefits.

Second, poor women suffer disproportionately from the use of abortion to indirectly target other social problems. Demographically, legal abortion is supported most strongly by the well-off, the white and the educated, and opposed most strongly by the poor, the minority and the less educated. Yet poor and minority women have a disproportionately high number of abortions compared to those better off financially. Abortion, first offered in the name of a "right" for the poor, soon becomes, in poor communities, one of the only choices or the only choice offered by society. Yet another terrible distinction develops between the haves and the have-nots.

In the most general terms, the entire phenomenon of using abortion—deemed a "tragedy" even by its supporters—to indirectly solve social problems is evidence of society's replacing "shame" with "shamelessness." We are tired of the guilt over our long term problems. We want instant solutions. We decide to opt for the quick-fix and evade the moral debate entirely.

## INDIVIDUALISM VS. COMMUNITARIANISM

Studies regularly show that, among abortion advocates, highest priority is accorded the values of "freedom" and "independence." Among pro-life advocates, the values of "the family" and "the common good" receive highest priority. Not surprisingly, therefore, the argument for legal abortion is often publicly articulated in absolutist, even crassly individualistic terms.

But the argument, made this way, also promotes individual autonomy itself as the all-important value. "It's not abortion we seek," say abortion advocates, "but the autonomy to *choose* it."

The decision to bear and raise a child is framed in the most individualistic terms. They say, the child is really a part of the mother's body. It is the woman, therefore, who must decide whether to "continue the pregnancy." And this decision flows from the "right of privacy"; neither the state, nor the father, nor the grandparents can counteract her decision. Framed in this way, there is no room for envisioning the woman and her child as the object of concern of the larger community. The community—including the child's father and grandparents—must stifle its natural concern until the mother gives the nod. Children are not a gift, and pregnant women are not objects of special care; rather children are primarily chosen objects, and pregnant women are autonomous agents who have chosen the hardship of childbearing in the exercise of their right of "privacy." With the abortion option continuously available, the community feels it can always rightfully say, "Why should we share our resources with you when we gave you every chance not to bring this burden into your life or ours?" Pope John Paul II's admonition, "We are our brothers' keepers!" (cf. Gen. 4:9) is ignored; childrearing is not appraised a matter of concern for the extended family and the caring community, but as solo flying for those who are deemed to have accepted freely all its consequences.

Some other outgrowths of the practice of legal abortion and the rhetoric supporting it include the following: the growing resentment of the introduction of "morality" into the public square, specifically as articulated by religious bodies (whether in sectarian or secular language); and the growing belief that there is no right or wrong sexual behavior, only bad consequences (sexually transmitted diseases, AIDS, pregnancy) of neutral sexual behavior; a growing willingness to view human beings not as ends in themselves, but as means to someone else's ends—exemplified by the burgeoning traffic in fetal body parts.

These are the most notorious future consequences I see from the continued widespread practice of abortion. They are substantiated by decades of experience with legal abortion around the world. The do not add up to a pretty future. Of course, there is no reason for despair; positive developments flowing from phenomena other than abortion will also constitute our future world. But legal abortion itself has had and can have no long term, life-giving consequences for our world.

# 9

## Abortion and Healing: A Pastoral Church Responds in Word and Sacrament

*Rev. Michael Mannion, S.T.L., M.A.*

The woman stood up tall and strong in the audience, in the midst of many. She had had an abortion. She was away from the Church for over twenty years. Her question after my presentation was sincere and insightful. My question to her came partly out of curiosity, partly out of admiration: "Why did you decide to come back to the Church? Where did you get the courage?" Her response was short, simple and from the heart: "I felt it was safe to come home." She was not saying the abortion was okay or in any form justified. Especially now, she knew too much about her life and life in the womb; had felt too much pain and hurt in the wake of her abortion; hungered too much for THE place within herself and among others where she could belong, be forgiven, be whole, feel and be at home. Now she knew from personal experience that the destruction of her child's life had not brought healing and peace to her own. As one author wrote, "You cannot guarantee your happiness . . . (even) at the cost of another's life." (Ellen Wilson Fielding, *The Human Life Review*, Summer, 1991, p. 22)

To some the Church is primarily an institution, but to others a community of faith; to some a serving community, to others a sacramental crossroads where each day life and death come together in symbol and reality: the place where a son or daughter is baptized, a deceased parent prayed for before the altar, sins forgiven and marriage bonds forged. Church is home.

For many the Church is the place of childhood memories and conflicting adult fears: "I once belonged; I don't belong now." "I know how set the church is against abortion. I'd like to go back. I can't." "My child didn't just die. I killed him. What the church stands for and who I am are too incompatible. Now I even feel uncomfortable driving by a church."

To all this, a pastoral and compassionate Church says, through the power and authority of Jesus Christ, "If there's a way to leave home—there's a way to come home. There's a way to be reconciled." The message comes across loud and clear in the 1984 words of Pope John Paul II:

> As we deduce from the parable of the Prodigal Son, reconciliation is a gift of God, an initiative on his part. We also rejoice in God through our Lord Jesus Christ, through whom we have now received our reconciliation. (Rom. 5:10; Col. 1:20) (Post-Synodal Apostolic Exhortation of His Holiness Pope John Paul II: "On Reconciliation and Penance—In the Mission of the Church Today")

The issue of reconciliation with God has its roots in the spiritual authority of the Church. Therapy and counseling may have led one to look above and grasp beyond the threshold of one's own pain and alienation, but it is only the Author of Life who ultimately has the power to heal the loss of life.

If the Church, through the power of the Spirit and in the name of the Father, cannot forgive abortion, then Christ's death on the cross 2,000 years ago was inadequate in love, in intensity, in power. And we know that is not so: "We also boast of God through our Lord Jesus Christ, through whom we have now received reconciliation" (Rom. 5:11).

The healing process is a journey of faith. One must believe Christ's sacrifice of love on the cross was enough to forgive *me* and *my sin.*

The distance between the two points, from alienation to coming home—for many a road paved with anger and depression, fear and frustration, denial and confrontation—is often an intense spiritual journey that begins with an emptiness marking not just the death of one's child, but also, in a sense, the death of the presence of one's God within one's self. The endings are many, comprising not a final point of arrival, but a process of growth and spiritual development through which one gains a true "head and heart" knowledge of Jesus Christ and a personal experience of his love. Through a YES to the call of His Church, one is enabled to continuously encounter and deepen the relationship with Christ in Sacrament, Word, and Community, or, as some would say, in Bread, Book, and Body. Yet those who are away from home must first hunger for it before they will return. They might first, unfortunately, settle for or even pursue substitutes in the form of alcohol and substance abuse, negative emotional and sexual relationships, and even intense and bitterly held commitments to causes and organizations that promote abortion and serve to expand the distance between one's own closeted or suppressed pain and the reality of one's daily life. Sometimes it takes a long time to learn the why and source of one's own pain, and an even longer time to face it.

As a church, we have seen our history riddled with moments of holiness and sinfulness, which should serve to make us all stand more humbly beneath the shadow of the Cross, ever recognizing our need for God's grace. As individuals, we know we all abort God's will in one way or another each day. This should only serve to make us more compassionate toward those who struggle to come home to their church. As Fr. John Dillon writes in his book, *A Path to Hope,* "Empathy for another rises out of the depths of our own brokenness and healing. 'You may call God love, you may call God goodness, but the best name for God is compassion,' writes the great mystic Meister Eckhart.' " It is a sobering thought to recognize that "we are all capable of that which we wish to heal," Fr. Dillon writes.

In the Catholic community there is a pastoral, scriptural and sacramental context to the post-abortion healing process. Through and within this framework, we as Church can share and call forth the fullness of one's relationship, experience, and identity with the Triune God: "God looks out for the return of his child, embraces him when he arrives and orders the banquet of the new meeting with which reconciliation is celebrated." ("On Reconciliation and Penance," p. 22). The aborted woman is not just to be tolerated when she returns home; she is to be welcomed. The Peters, Augustines and countless others throughout history remind us how powerfully God uses those who were once broken to be his instruments of healing for others of his children, yet to return. Indeed, some of our most effective and spiritually empowered leaders in the pro-life, post-abortion healing movement today are those who were once not just victims but advocates of abortion.

The pastoral approach is ever mindful of the need for deep conversion as a prerequisite for reconciliation, lest the sacramental experience, especially, be temporary and mechanical. Yet all this must take place within the context of a loving and welcoming atmosphere. If the context or texture of one's reintroduction to church is not warm, welcoming, friendly, and safe, the individual will often not remain long enough to "investigate" the content or text of the whole healing process and the message of God's love itself. Some seem afraid that love and acceptance of the aborted woman or father of the aborted child will send a message of compromise. This fear can be addressed by the recognition that between the two counterproductive extremes of condemnation and condonement lies compassion and conviction. To condemn the aborted woman or condone the abortion will not only accomplish little, but will also serve to block God's healing graces through the Church. To show compassion to one who comes, usually after a long and painful experience of the traumatic aftereffects of abortion, as well as conviction concerning the sacredness of all human life in the womb, further helping to elucidate the cause of the pain, serves to further God's healing plan for his children. As the ancient maxim says, "In what is doubtful, freedom; in what is necessary, unity; in all things, charity."

Permeating the healing process is the constant stress on the need for ongoing conversion, interspersed with a comprehensive examination of one's life motives, agendas, actions, relationships, commitments, and hurts. Needless to say, the abortion did not take place in a vacuum. If the pain of the abortion is to be healed, all that is a part of it—persons, places, and things that were conducive to it—must be spiritually addressed as well, in the light of God's plan for one's life *now*: "What must I change, turn from, turn to, here and now that I may fully accept and experience God's healing grace and reconciliation in my life?" If a past abortion is addressed only in a "freeze-frame" examination of one's life, it is very possible that another will someday follow. To put it rather succinctly, "In the decision making, vulnerable times of my life, who are those persons, what are those things, that cried out for death rather than life?"

An honest response to the above questions as well as a deep-seated commitment to their answers leads to a true metanoia and penance as well. This all happens within the pastoral context of the "call to come home": "If we link penance with the metanoia which the Synoptics refer to, it means the inmost change of heart under the influence of the Word of God and in the perspective of the Kingdom. But penance also means changing one's life in harmony with the change of heart" ("On Reconciliation and Penance," p. 10).

The pastoral flows into the scriptural when the abortion victim composes his or her story. It is helpful if at first the story is written, then told, and perhaps even retold, each time identifying its events with comparable scriptural events. The aborted woman, for example, may be able to identify with the figures of biblical history who also struggled to be faithful to God—and give life—when so many forces around them were crying out for death: Abraham, Moses,

David. The women of biblical history—Sarah, Ruth, Esther, to name
but a few, may be powerful inspirations as well—not just for their
successes, but for their fears and failures as well. When—how—
why? did I feel like that person of the Bible? How can my present
insights interwoven with God's grace here and now help me to be
reconciled with God, myself, my neighbor, the whole of creation?

We are generally as free as those we can't forgive. The
aborted woman's spiritual, psychological and even physical freedom
may have much to do with her ability to forgive those who were a
part of her abortion. All those who encouraged her or even remained
silent in the midst of it may be a significant part of her journey to
healing and reconciliation. She may even have to forgive her baby
for coming at "the wrong time." A boyfriend or husband, doctor or
nurse, parent or friend—all may be part of the cycle of pain and
unforgiveness, all will be part of her conversion of heart. Each may
someday need to journey his or her own healing path home to the
Father as well.

Conversion of heart usually precedes intellectual faith convictions. Abbott David Geraets once said that Augustine believed that
we experience love before revelation and not the other way around.
We don't "think ourselves" into a new way of living, we experience
and "live" ourselves into "a new way of thinking." ("Catechesis and
Christian Renwewal," talk for School for Spiritual Directors, Pecos
Benedictine Monastery, Pecos, N.M., January, 1989.) Conversion of
heart, always initiated by God's grace, often through contact with a
loving and compassionate pastoral Church, leads to a hunger for the
content of revelation, and then to a transformation of the whole person. Transformation brings with it empowerment. Then a healing
Christ continues to reach out in the world of our day through one
who herself was broken.

The woman or man wounded by abortion comes to the experience and reality of reconciliation with God, self, and others personally but not privately: "The first means of this salvific action is that
of prayer. It is certain that the Blessed Virgin, Mother of Christ and
of the Church, and the Saints who have now reached the end of
their earthly journey and possess God's glory, sustain by their inter-
cession their brethren who are on pilgrimage through the world, in
the commitment to conversion, to faith, to getting up again after
every fall, to acting in order to help the growth of communion and
peace in the world." (Pope Paul VI, Allocution at the Closing of the

Third Session of the Second Vatican Ecumenical Council, 21 November 1964: AAS 56 (1964), 1015-1018.)

The Communion of Saints not only prays for the women and men who struggle to return home to the Church. They also provide a powerful model of faith as they struggle. The lessons of their lives help the victims of abortion here and now to make their suffering an act of love, to give their lives a vision of paschal mystery, through which all that happens to us can be seen through the eyes of the life, death, and resurrection of Jesus Christ.

Archbishop Fulton J. Sheen once said, "The greatest tragedy is not what people suffer but that they have no one whom they love to whom they can offer their cross." The healing process expands and stretches our capacity to love and be loved—by our God, by ourselves, by others.

As is written in the book *Abortion and Healing,* (Michael T. Mannion, [Kansas City, MO: Sheed & Ward, rev. ed. 1992]), "One does not come to (an understanding of) Resurrection by bypassing the Cross."

When abortion is seen for what it is, especially by the victims of it, its reality is obvious: Abortion is violence often masquerading as compassion. So many honestly believe it to be a solution and fail to see it for what it is and does. Time reveals that grief is a logical consequence of death and that "you will always remember the child you never knew." This fact has serious spiritual as well as emotional implications. (The experience of God's grace and love in the grieving process can not only heal the abortion but open one's heart to a whole new faith vision of life as well.) In terms of the forgiveness and healing process, the Cross provides a powerful bond between the victims of violence, especially the aborted woman, and Mary—the Mother of Jesus.

Jesus was nailed to the cross by the sins and violence of a world that was threatened and fearful of its very source of life. Mary stood at the foot of the cross with an unwavering faith that lacked all consolation.

The aborted child is also nailed to a cross, created by the same violent and sinful world, that claims it has no place or room for a new child. A grieving mother stands at the foot of this cross as well, having herself been deluded by that world into denying her very nurturing nature and becoming a participant in the destruction of her own child.

The relationship between the two—Mary, the Mother of Jesus, and the mother of the aborted child—is formed and forged through the Death and Resurrection of Jesus that, by the power of the Holy Spirit, reaches down through the Church in human history. It is, in a sense, the arms of Jesus, reaching down from the Cross, one embracing his Mother, the other embracing the repentant aborted woman, that brings them both together.

The aborted woman can thank Jesus for the friendship, consolation and support of his Mother. To quote the words of Cardinal James A. Hickey, Archbishop of Washington:

> 'Mary's darkness at the foot of the cross was a dark night of faith; the darkness that engulfed the onlookers was a darkness of unbelief." ("Mary—Mother of the Redeemer," 1988)

It is often this darkness of unbelief, despair and hopelessness that pervades and overshadows the life of the aborted woman. She can draw tremendous strength and healing for her spiritual journey from a personal relationship with the Mother of Jesus. Surely Mary can especially identify with the fears of the young and pregnant teenager. Although the origin of life within her was different, the depth of her compassion could not but reach out to another who knew the loss of her child and regretted it. Together they look at the Cross; together they look beyond it and see the open tomb.

God the Father used the crucified Christ as the main vehicle to heal an aborted world. Jesus, through his Spirit, used the crucified aborted child as the main vehicle to hear the aborted woman. Healing and holding, reconciliation and reunion, remembering and dreaming go hand-in-hand.

Like the repentant Roman soldier, the woman, in the midst of her grieving process, stands at the foot of the Cross. Looking beyond the Cross, she sees the open tomb and knows Christ is risen and her baby will arise. Our faith, in its fullness, promises us not only reconciliation with the Author of Life but reunion with the child that was lost. Forgiveness and the communion of saints provide a powerful vision of a world to come in the midst of God's love here and now."

All of this is possible because of "a love more powerful than sin, stronger than death" (Pope John Paul II, Encyclical *Dives in Misericordia*, 8;15: AAS 72 (1980), 1203-1207; 1231).

Recognizing that "what is pastoral is not opposed to what is doctrinal" ("On Reconciliation and Penance," p. 93), the Church recognizes that each sacrament, "over and above its own proper grace, is also a sign of penance and reconciliation."

Through all the sacraments, a loving God who created the world uses bread, wine, oil and water to mediate his presence in the world. By doing this He basically proclaims, "The world I created is worth redeeming and saving." In the Incarnation of the Word made flesh, Jesus Christ, God, in the most profound way, "uses flesh to save flesh," and states, "The world I created is worth suffering and dying for to save." The sacraments are not just a doctrine to be believed but a whole way of life to be lived; not just statements of credal fact, but a vision and way of life to live by and through which to relate.

The abortion victim is called home to be a part of this whole vision once again. It is here that the pastoral and the doctrinal not only do not conflict, but actually blend beautifully.

This vision stretches from baptism, where one is reminded of his or her initiation into the Body of Christ through the call to identify with the life, death, and resurrection of Jesus, as well as one's purification from original sin.

Those wounded by abortion can find particular solace in this reality—for in this baptismal relationship as a child of God lies their very identity. The abortion victim, for example, is not an "aborted woman," but a woman—created, loved, and redeemed by God, who has had an abortion. In the dark moments of despair, she may well be tempted to define herself by what she's done: abortion. A loving Father wishes to define her by who she is: a child of God, on her way home, rather than by what she has done. Baptism reminds her that God wishes her to be part of his family, in the fullest way.

As she remembers baptism and recognizes that her hunger for Eucharist will lead her through the transforming experience of penance and reconciliation, she will not only remember the call of faith of the early Christians, but hers, in conformity with theirs, as well.

Their faith had to face the fact, "Christ has died." She must now admit and accept, "My baby has died—not an illusion but a fact that demands, in the here and now, that I let go."

Their faith was given new hope when they knew and proclaimed, "Christ has risen." Though the victim of the new technological Herods of our day who demand the death of a child that an industry may flourish, though a false promise is attached that the world will be bettered by the death of a child, a grieving mother is given new hope in the firm faith that "my baby will arise." The death of the victim is conquered by the Lord of Life, who will share His victory with "my child."

Finally, their faith was empowered when they recognized that Christ would not abandon them, for the age of the Spirit was upon them and then "Christ will come again." A sorrowful mother now knows, "Yes, Christ will come again, and when He does, He'll be carrying my baby in his arms."

In the Church the experience of penance and reconciliation is particularly embodied in the Sacrament of Reconciliation. The priest, as the minister of this sacrament, acts in "persona Christi." "This power to 'forgive sins' Jesus confers through the Holy Spirit, upon ordinary men, themselves subject to the snare of sin, namely his Apostles: 'Receive the Holy Spirit. Whose sins you shall forgive, they are forgiven; whose sins you shall retain, they are retained' " (John 20:22; Matt. 18:18). ("On Reconciliation and Penance," p. 108, 109).

The priest, in the person of Christ, is called to relate to the penitent as brother (also a sinner), Shepherd, (seeking the lost sheep), Physician (who heals and comforts), Master (who teaches the truth and reveals the ways of God), and to some extent, even Judge (who judges according to the truth and not according to appearances). The words of Augustine are important: "I wish to heal, not accuse."

To those who doubt the power of the sacrament, and for whom healing relies upon faith, the appropriate question is not "Can a man forgive sins?" but "Can the Church forgive sins?" For a given priest's authority to forgive sins rests not in himself but with the Church community that empowers and ordains him to do so, in the name of the Church Jesus founded and with his authority behind it.

Today, many refer to this sacrament as the Sacrament of Reconciliation, choosing to name it not by one of its parts (e.g., confession, penance) but by one of its principal effects, for by it one is reconciled to God, others, and self.

The experience of this sacrament may well be one of the most powerful healing moments of an abortion victim's life, for through it countless moments of her personal history can converge before the common embrace of a healing God.

Before the celebration of the Sacrament, the aborted woman can draw her thoughts together from a journal she's kept, and the personal story she's written. She may write a letter to the child she's aborted, calling the child by name. Through the abortion she has said, "You are not my child." In her heart of hearts, she will soon hear her child say to her, "You are my mother." Her child, now seeing the face of God, cannot but forgive her. Her child's prayers for her are another part of her journey home. She may prepare for the Sacrament by choosing a special scripture passage which speaks to her of her own faith journey back to the Lord and his Church. Luke 15—The Loving Father—is a common choice. The time for the celebration of the Sacrament will be one when the aborted woman knows, "I want to be forgiven. I know God wants to forgive me. I wish to say yes to His call to a change of heart and changes in my life. I know God will forgive me." The priest may suggest a date immediately preceding a special feast: Christmas, Easter, for example. For some, even Mother's Day is a special time to receive one's second "First Holy Communion." During the actual celebration of the Sacrament of Reconciliation, the following elements will be present:

*Confession*: To express our sins before the representative of the Church community, to hear our own words, thus truly admitting of the sins for which we seek forgiveness. "The individual confession also has the value of a sign: a sign of the meeting of the sinner with the mediation of the Church in the person of the minister" ("On Reconciliation and Penance," p. 120-121). Considering the fact that all sin is social in nature, this element is especially important in the case of abortion. In abortion, a child of God, made in his image and likeness, has died. A mother has chosen to say no to the gift of life. All of creation is the poorer for this. In the rejection of the gift is found the rejection of the Giver. Her subjective culpability may vary, dependent on the degree of full consent and serious reflection, but the objective gravity of the act cannot be disputed. A human life has been lost. The Author of Life must heal the loss of life. His love is greater than death. By the act of confessing, one, in fact, says, "I wish to draw near to the power of that love."

"The confession of sins therefore cannot be reduced to a mere attempt at psychological liberation, even though it corresponds to that legitimate and natural need, inherent in the human heart, to open oneself to another. It is a liturgical act, solemn in its dramatic nature, yet humble and sober in the grandeur of its meaning. It is the act of the Prodigal Son who returns to his father and is welcomed by him with the kiss of peace. It is an act of honesty and courage. It is an act of entrusting oneself, beyond sin, to the mercy that forgives" ("On Reconciliation and Penance," p. 121).

For the abortion victim who has had the experience of numerous visits to therapists or counselors, who may have helped in many ways but have not had the authority to assure one of God's forgiveness nor the ability to proclaim God's peace to one who is tortured, this element is particularly crucial. The sacrament is not therapy, nor is therapy the sacrament, but they can coincide to work together for the common goal of emotional and spiritual healing. Grace builds on nature; grace works through nature.

*Contrition*: To recognize our sinfulness as an opportunity to reestablish and strengthen our relationship with God out of a bond of love rather than a fear of punishment; to be truly and genuinely sorry. Contrition is "the beginning and the heart of conversion . . . a clear and decisive rejection of the sin committed, together with a resolution not to commit it again." True contrition is extremely liberating, for it frees us to turn (convert; 'metanoia') to God and accept his love. For many broken by abortion, the gift of forgiveness has always awaited them. Contrition has freed them to accept it, sometimes breaking through after years of self-hatred and feelings of despicableness. Contrition and conversion go hand-in-hand. Once one stands humbly before the Lord and says, "I'm sorry. I was wrong," one never stands in the same place again. One is changed, no longer looking backward to despair, but forward to hope. One still stands at the foot of the cross, but now one looks beyond it to see the open tomb. "That which has broken me has also transformed me." In the mystery of the paschal, those who erected the cross—are saved by it.

*Penance*: To commit ourselves to prayer and action that expresses our spirit of remorse and regret for past sins and our commitment to a changed future. This penance, or satisfaction, is "not a price that one pays for the sin absolved and for the forgiveness obtained." That price was paid on Good Friday 2,000 years ago by the blood of the Lord. The penance is a sign of a new life, not to be reduced to mere formulas but "should consist of acts of worship, charity, mercy, or reparation." It is often helpful to ask the abortion victim to do a penance with both a meditative and apostolic element. The meditative aspect may involve a particular scripture passage and even the entire book or gospel from which it is taken. The apostolic aspect may involve a commitment to donate volunteer hours to an organization that is life-giving (e.g., soup kitchen, homeless shelter, handicapped). Some may wish to give themselves to work with unwed mothers, or other pro-life activities. This is acceptable and even commendable as long as it is done not to 'earn God's love and for-giveness' but to thank Him for it.

*Absolution:* To accept the Church's proclamation of healing and rec-onciliation, for who we are, for what we've done, by the authority of the Church, rooted in history and stretching back to the death and resurrection of Jesus himself. With the powerful convergence of "I absolve you" and the imposition of the hand and the sign of the Cross, the contrite and converted sinner comes into contact with the power and mercy of God. The sign of "resurrection" from "spiritual death" is renewed once again. This is not just a voice coming from within, nor a therapeutic statement rooted in theories and formu-las—this is the voice of the living, resurrected God speaking from the gibbet of the Cross—"Father, forgive them"—to the day of the Open Tomb—"Peace be with you"—to the humbled heart of an aborted woman or a grieving father who now says, "Lord, I too am unworthy, but thank you, thank you, thank you for loving me." This is the voice coming through a human sinful priest speaking for the Church that is both sinful and holy—Jesus's body and voice throug-hout history. Even though the action of God's forgiveness may oc-cur, in some cases, long before the feeling of forgiveness is experi-enced, the fact remains the same forgiveness is given as God's gift. For our feelings are a part of our faith, but our faith goes far be-yond our feelings. As our faith grows stronger, we are better able to forgive ourselves as God has forgiven us. It is now that the pas-toral, the scriptural, and the sacramental all begin to come together. A compassionate Church reaches out with the story of its history, stretching back beyond the upper room to the darkest places of the many lives of the here and now. In it all we see that the God of Revelation is the God of Liberation. The more we allow his saving work in human history, salvation history, and *our* history to touch our lives, the more free we are to be ourselves and live our lives as people of reconciliation and healing: God's instruments to liberate ourselves and others from the divisions, bondages, delusions, and decisions of death that incarcerate us.

And those who come forth, abortion victims among them, are not unlike the Lazarus of old:

Christ spoke: "Take away the stone." Through loving pastoral outreach, our Church is called to "take away the stones" that block the broken from coming home to the Lord and his Church.

"Lazarus, come out!" he cried. Our Scriptures—rooted in the authority of the Word of God itself—are a constant cry—invitation—to come out of ourselves, from the darkness of death to the safety and beauty of God's healing light.

"Unbind him and let him go free" (John 11). Our sacraments are vehicles for and proclamations of God's new life in freedom. We can conquer and leave the tomb of spiritual death and despair.

"I am the bread of life; whoever comes to me will never hunger, and whoever believes in me will never thirst" (John 6:35). People are free when they are in touch with and respond to the source of their lives.

The Church, then, must be that home—here—in which the aborted woman can rediscover, or perhaps discover for the first time, the goodness of who she is beneath the evil of what she's done.

And as the Bread of Life is taken in that long-awaited and longed-for Eucharist, a grieving mother can remember her child who was aborted, but also look forward to a child that she will one day hold, when, together, they will share the home of the Father.


## ACCEPTED IN THE BELOVED

I don't have to accomplish great things to be accepted by God
    but because I am accepted I can accomplish great things
I don't have to succeed to please God
    but because I please God I can succeed
I don't have to love others for God to love me
    but because He loves me I love others
I don't have to serve to be valued by God
    but because I am valued I can serve
I don't have to prove myself worthy
    but because I am worthy I am approved
I don't have to obey to earn God's love
    but because God loves me I obey
I don't have to suffer greatly before I am healed
    but because He suffered greatly I am healed
I don't have to demonstrate great faith before mountains will move
    but because of his faithfulness mountains will move
Since You are, therefore I am.

—Carol L. Piles[*]

*Piles, Carol L., *The Journal of Christian Healing*. Vol. 13, no. 2, Summer 1991.

# 10

## Post-Abortion Trauma and the Adolescent

### Wanda Franz, Ph.D.

---

DEVELOPMENTAL IMPLICATIONS OF ABORTION

In the United States, one-third of all abortions are to teenagers and one-half are to women 24 years of age and under. If there are developmental problems associated with abortion for these young women, then the implications for health care in this country may be very significant. Unfortunately, it is impossible to say what constitutes the age of maturity when developmental problems could be said to be resolved. For example, research such as that discussed below demonstrates that a majority of high school students show immature cognitive functioning. On the other hand, it is likely that even college students continue to show signs of cognitive immaturity. Ideally, it should be possible, when doing research, to measure cognitive maturity independently to see if it is associated with sexuality and abortion decision making. Such research has not yet been undertaken.

It could be argued that there are many "adult adolescents" who have reached an age where maturity should be well developed but who have simply never grown up. It is possible that there is a disproportionate number of immature adults to be found among abortion survivors. If such a relationship were found to be true it could be due to either the adult immaturity causing the self-involved actions, such as abortion, with consequent problems, or the immaturity may be caused and exacerbated by the abortion experience. At this time there is limited evidence about the developmental characteristics of the aborted woman.

There are many questions pertaining to developmental issues that can be asked, for example: Do some developmental factors make a woman more prone to post-abortion problems? Do developmental factors affect her perception of the abortion experience? Do developmental factors affect the course of post-abortion trauma? Do developmental factors have an impact on the methods used to assist the woman with post-abortion trauma? Unfortunately, we do not have definitive answers to all of these questions. However, a brief overview of the developmental characteristics of adolescents compared with mature women offers some tentative hypotheses about differences. The following sections represent an initial attempt to do this. The first section addresses the research on adolescent functioning and the differences between adolescents and adults in their responses to abortion. This is followed by an analysis of well-established and well-known theories about adolescent functioning, including applications to post-abortion trauma.

RESEARCH EVIDENCE

Developmental psychologists are aware of the limitations in the ability of adolescents to analyze, evaluate and effectively respond to important decision making situations in their lives. There is clear evidence that the cognitive limitations of adolescents have an impact on their sexual decision making (Franz, 1987 & 1989). One example of such limitations is a study by Kirby (1985). He has found that after taking traditional sexuality education courses, adolescents perform well on tests of knowledge. However, they give evidence of not being able to use the information they have acquired. They can correctly answer questions about the menstrual cycle, but if asked at what point in the menstrual cycle intercourse has the greatest chance of leading to pregnancy, the majority will give a wrong answer. In other words, adolescents may have all of the necessary information but be unable to process and organize it. This is predicted by the developmental theory of Jean Piaget.

In addition, among adolescents there is a high proportion of immature individuals. The reasons for this may be found in a number of different developmental theories, especially that of Erik Erikson. Erikson argued that adult maturity evolves from the development of the person's sense of self-identity. He claims that the task of adolescence is to establish that sense of identity. Adolescents are very prone to acquiring low self-esteem during this critical period. For this reason, sexual decisions can have important developmental implications for adolescents. Thus, based upon both theory and research, it is possible to predict that adolescents will make more inadequate sexuality and abortion decisions then mature adults and that they will have more difficulty coping with the results of their decisions.

Few studies have been done which compare adolescents with adults in their ability to cope with abortion. Campbell, Franco and Jurs (1988) found that teenagers were significantly more likely to report parental marital difficulties, to attempt suicide following abortion, to have severe nightmares following abortion and to be less likely to report being coerced into their decision to abort. In addition, the adolescent aborters had significantly higher scores on scales measuring antisocial traits, paranoia, drug abuse, and psychotic delusions. Thus, this study found clear evidence that adolescents have more problems following abortion than adults.

Franz and Reardon (1992) analyzed the post-abortion effects of 252 women from support group organizations for women suffering negative effects of abortion. The sample was separated into those having their abortion under the age of 20 and those having them over the age of 20. A series of t-test comparisons were made between adolescents and older women. Adolescents were significantly more likely to report greater severity of psychological stress, to feel they were misinformed during pre-abortion counseling, and to prefer to keep the baby. They were also significantly more likely to have a long time-lag between the abortion and the survey, to have abortions later in term, and to be less satisfied with services at the time of abortion. In contract to the study by Campbell, Franco and Jurs (1988), they were more apt to feel forced into the abortion.

These data give the impression of adolescents who do not want to abort but feel they must because there are few other options. This is typical for young people who generally have diminished actual control over their lives. However, the lack of control appears to be associated with longer periods spent in denial and with greater psychological stress. Thus, adolescents may be at greater risk for problems following abortion than older women. It is interesting that the adolescents were more likely to report receiving misinformation. This could be due to the fact that adolescents have a greater difficulty in understanding and integrating complex information, such as that involving a decision to abort. It is possible that correct information was given but the adolescents did not understand it. It is also likely that adolescent cognitive immaturity might hinder adequate counseling efforts.

Other findings from this study have implications for adolescents. A report of "worsened self-image" was significantly related to being least satisfied with the choice at the time of the abortion, to being least satisfied with the services at the time of abortion, to feeling extreme pressure to have the abortion, to having the least well thought-out decision, to believing they had received the least information and to very much wanting to keep the baby. Since adolescents are so heavily involved with establishing a self-image, the possibility of the abortion experience to act as a factor in "worsened self-image" is of great importance. It is possible that the development of an identity could be delayed by the abortion.

Correlations were run which provide some additional information. Age at the time of the abortion was significantly correlated with "time since the abortion." Thus, the younger the woman when she had her abortion, the longer the time until she sought help for post-abortion problems. Age at the time of the abortion was also correlated with satisfaction today. That is, the younger the woman when she had her abortion, the less satisfied she was later. These data suggest that the teenager is apt to be in denial longer than the older woman and to be more negatively effected by the abortion.

The two studies comparing adolescents with adults in their reactions to abortions (Campbell, Franco & Jurs, 1988; Franz & Reardon, 1992) both found that the effects of the abortion experience were more negative for the adolescents. These studies provide some confirmation of the expectation that adolescents are cognitively immature and have greater difficulty making adequate decisions. In addition, Franz and Reardon (1992) found that adolescents report negative experiences with pre-abortion counseling. In retrospect, they report more negative feelings about the decision making process than adult women. The counseling procedures appeared to be important to the outcome of the adolescent's self-image. It appears to be important that adolescents not be pressured into the abortion decision, and that they feel they have the time and information before they make a decision. In order to understand these findings, it is necessary to examine some of the theories about adolescent development. The sections that follow will examine adolescent body image, adolescent egocentrism, and concrete operational thought.

## ADOLESCENT BODY IMAGE

Adolescents strongly depend on environmental feedback to establish their sense of who they are and what impression they make. Broughton (1978), in analyzing the development of our concept of truth and knowledge, described development from the preschool years to young adulthood. He found that young children have a unitary notion of the body and mind, with truth coming from contact with the environment. This orientation evolves into a mind-body dichotomy in adolescence, which Broughton called early dualism (beginning at age 12) and dualistic (beginning at age 18). According to his analysis, at around the age of 12 years, individuals begin to see the mind and body as both capable of contact with the "real world" and as capable of producing knowledge. The body takes in scientifically oriented, factual knowledge but the mind takes in social knowledge, which it obtains through social awareness of others. This awareness of social issues is part of the maturing cognitive abilities of the adolescent and was not available to the younger child.

The inner self comes to have more importance for the adolescent then the outer self. The self is conceived as

> The inner side, the mind mostly. How the mind works. Because your body is your outside but yourself is more your mind. . . . There are physical things that everybody has, and they are still a part of you, but a more minor part (Broughton, 1978).

Thus, there is a split between the "real" inner self and the social appearance or personality through which the self is presented to others. Understanding this difference leads to great confusion. Given the confusion, being yourself can be very difficult:

> Being yourself, acting natural . . . not phony. . . . The self is something you want people to see . . . everybody is really phony, but you're trying to act natural. The mind . . . is what you really think inside you . . . and sometimes you're scared to say (Broughton, 1978).

However, validation from others is essential in providing the adolescent with the information about what is truly the real, natural self. The truth about yourself "comes from people wanting it to be truth all the time" or "You need the support of someone saying 'that's good'" (Broughton, 1978).

By age 18 this dualism is complete, and the young person perceives that truth is what the majority agrees to be the conventional reality. Scientific knowledge is conceived of as physical reality, but the mind has a distinct reality based upon commonly agreed upon perceptions. This level of reality allows the individual to have self-understanding characterized by a sense of individuation which is a permanent, unique, transcendent personality. At this level the subject explains the meaning of the self:

> The body for me is just an appearance, is just a shadow. It's the living force inside you; you know, the ideas that emanate, that are the self (Broughton, 1978).

During this stage, the young person is reluctant to condemn "mere, external behavior" in another person. They will argue that even though the person's behavior may be "bad," the person is "really good on the inside." Without the ability to integrate mind and body, the adolescent finds it very difficult to understand that if people persist in lying, they will ultimately become liars, or if they persist in fornicating, they will become fornicators. When adults express concerns about such behavior, adolescents are apt to view them as "narrow," "bigoted," or, worst of all, "judgmental."

Another important factor here is that the adolescent personality heavily depends on external sources for assurance of its qualities and characteristics. However, the young person has a strong sense of dualism: an inner me and an external me. At this age, it is possible for the person to be aware of an internal "unique, special me" being covered up by an external "proper me." They express frustration that the "true inner me" is not given proper recognition; hence the need to engage in antisocial activities to goad parents and influential adults into a closer examination of their "real" inner qualities.

This tendency in young people has important implications for post-abortion counseling. If a teenager has had an abortion, she may be covering up this fact as a part of her hated inner reality. She may perceive all of her interactions with concerned others as superficial and not involving her real self. She may struggle to maintain the separation of the two elements of her being, while at the same time desiring integration. She may have difficulty accepting responsibility for the needs and problems of her inner self, claiming that her proper, external self didn't agree to the irresponsible actions.

On the other hand, she may perceive the abortion to be something that happened to the minor, unimportant, outer self. Thus, the adolescent is in a position to ignore the importance of the abortion, since it has not touched the essential "inner self." This attitude could produce the characteristic pattern of teens in which they appear to go through the abortion without any problems and with hardly a backward glance. For this immature person, the abortion can be inconsequential. It is possible that the process of maturing helps trigger knowledge and understanding that forces the young person to grow up. It is possible that the developmental process could be linked to the breaking of denial regarding the seriousness of the abortion experience. That is, the young woman must first go through the process of changing her view of herself as someone who has merely "had an abortion" to someone who is the "destroyer of her child."

This adolescent duality will ultimately evolve into what Broughton called "relativity" in which all reality is relative to the context, and knowledge is self-constructed, based on reflections of the thinking of others. During this stage, there is no rationality. It is a transition stage for the next level which is the dialectic process of mind and body in constructive tension, functioning by separate laws but serving each other. This stage may evolve into a stage where a higher reality of mind becomes dominant; however, Broughton did not observe this directly.

## ADOLESCENT EGOCENTRISM

This was defined by Elkind (1976) as a stage in which the young person is so taken up with her new awareness of herself and her inner reality that it overwhelms her ability to focus on external events. Her social environment has reality for her only in so far as it provides her with feedback about her own personality. She misinterprets many social interactions as being directed entirely toward her inner reality. She cannot conceive of other people having needs and problems which may be motivating their behavior. She sees everything in terms of her own agency and causation.

For example, teenagers are often so self-conscious that they believe others will see exactly what they see in themselves. So the appearance of a new pimple may make an adolescent so overwhelmed with discomfort that she believes everyone sees it as clearly as she does, and interprets it as negatively as she does. Its presence causes her to be shy and uncomfortable in social situations. Yet her companions may never have noticed the new blemish. She assumes that everyone else takes it as seriously as she does.

Every action is carried out in order to see how others respond to it. Clothes are chosen to see what response they will bring in others (shock, approval, envy, etc.). The same system applies in interpersonal relations. The date to the school prom is chosen to enhance prestige with the group and to boost the ego. Dating during the adolescent years is carried out more to discover the identity of the self then of the date.

The young couple will spend hours preparing for the evening out. The clothes will be carefully chosen and the hair correctly combed. And when these young people meet, they will look into each other's eyes and see—not the other person, but the response to all the effort they have made. Like looking into a mirror, they see only themselves. They both have a need to receive affirmation. They have no understanding of a mutual relationship or of giving of themselves in unselfish love. However, this is entirely appropriate, since it is the developmental task to come to a better understanding of self. Once the self is fully grasped, it is then possible to establish a truly mature, mutual relationship with another person.

For the teenager who has had an abortion, this orientation can give a very distorted view of the causative factors affecting her behavior. She may be inclined to blame others for her behavior, because she perceives them as functioning only for her. For example, she isn't responsible for getting pregnant. It's her mother's fault for not providing her with contraception, etc. It will be particularly difficult for the adolescent to accept responsibility for her own decision to have an abortion and, consequently, for any problems that occur afterward.

One feature of this stage of adolescent egocentrism is particularly troublesome for those working with teenagers. That is the tendency of teens to see themselves as invulnerable. Elkind (1976) calls this the "personal fable," in which the adolescent believes herself to be protected from negative events. She sees herself as so special that the laws of probability don't apply to her. Thus, she can have sex without using contraception because "only other people have unplanned pregnancies." She can argue for having an abortion because physical and psychological problems only occur in other people.

The girl who has had an abortion may find it very difficult to admit to having any psychological problems. She will be inclined to blame others for her unhappiness, because she couldn't possibly be a victim of such problems. She will deny that she has a problem or that she could develop one. If she is engaging in self-destructive behavior, she will deny that the root cause may be her abortion experience.

## CONCRETE OPERATIONAL THOUGHT

Young people and many adults function at the level of concrete operational thought, as identified by Piaget (1954). Thinking at this level is characterized by concrete, short-term thinking without any ability to formalize abstract, long-term solutions or outcomes. The concrete operator cannot follow a cause and effect line of reasoning if it is abstract and hypothetical. Thus, the adolescent will not be able to see herself as responsible for long-term consequences of actions, which she cannot actually experience.

The young person who has had an abortion finds it very difficult to accept responsibility for her actions. She sees herself as a victim of circumstances, not able to realize that she has made decisions that have resulted in bad consequences. She is not conscious of making a decision; it just happened to her. Since she didn't intend to get pregnant, "It just happened." Therefore, the consequences are not her responsibility. She did not consciously decide to get pregnant; therefore, she has no responsibility for the baby. Obviously such thinking allows the young woman to deny her responsibility and prevents resolution of guilt-related problems.

## IDENTITY VS. IDENTITY CONFUSION

Erikson postulated that the adolescent's goal is to establish a sense of self-identity. If she does not complete this task adequately, she will be forced to enter into the responsibilities of adulthood with a poorly developed sense of personal identity. Erikson (1980) argued that future healthy development of intimate relationships would be hindered by failure during this stage. It is quite possible that when a woman has an abortion, she is forced to create protective walls of denial to prevent herself from facing the reality of the action. The effort to deny the abortion is enhanced by the many mechanisms that are present in adolescent thinking, such as confusion of means and ends, adolescent egocentrism, and mind-body dualities. Maintenance of this type of thinking prevents the development of true personal identity. The abortion event itself may contribute to a delay in the development of true identify, which thwarts future growth and development.

Bernstein (1980) has shown that in healthy development, the adolescent begins to define herself in terms of social personality characteristics which include the acceptance of rules and social standards and the search for stable personality characteristics. These new characteristics ultimately make it possible for the young person to take responsibility for her own self-motivating actions, which signals a shift to maturity. This process may be short-circuited by the abortion decision, which cannot be integrated adequately into the maturing personality.

## COUNSELING ADOLESCENTS

An examination of the effects of an adolescent decision to abort suggests that it can have a devastating impact on the young person's ability to mature and grow in the normal way. The adolescent is naturally inclined to be self-involved and egocentric. These characteristics tend to predispose a teenager to have an abortion. The adolescent is not able to conceptualize the long-range implications of the abortion decision or to take responsibility for them; thus she is in an excellent position to deny responsibility for her actions and simultaneously deny the negative aftereffects of the abortion. The teenage aborter is in a position to engage in abortion easily with little immediate evidence of negative aftereffects because she can so easily deny all true personal involvement. She can blame the abortion on the influence of others on her inner personality, which can be easily covered up by the greater reality of her day-to-day physical life.

It is possible that the breaking of denial requires the maturing of the individual to the point where she has progressed to a mature developmental level so that self-control and self-responsibility allow for realistic assessment of her actions. It is possible that the delay between the abortion event and the emergence of post-abortion syndrome is related to developmental changes in the individual woman. She needs time to grow and change before she can face the responsibility of her action. To encourage the adolescent to abort may, in fact, lead to delays in normal maturational processes.

Adolescents are clearly incapable of making thoughtful long-term decisions about their unplanned pregnancies. The difficulty they have is reflected in their reports of dissatisfaction with the pre-abortion counseling they received (Franz & Reardon, 1992). However, it is also clear that pre-abortion counseling by agencies referring for or providing abortions is universally poor and, in most cases, virtually nonexistent. This poor quality is particularly devastating to adolescents who have unique, developmental needs.

Clearly, adolescents need more time to evaluate the effects abortion could have on their lives. They need specific guidance throughout the counseling process to encourage logical analysis, assure that the long-term effects are considered and to apply rational and analytical conclusions.

It is unlikely that those providing pre-abortion counseling at abortion facilities have been trained in adolescent development and have sufficient knowledge to be able to help the adolescent overcome egocentric thinking. In fact, it is against their economic interest to do so.

Women suffering from post-abortion trauma tend to report feelings of being pressured into the abortion against their will, of being victimized by a lack of information and support (Franz & Reardon, 1992). Because adolescents have the greatest difficulty understanding whatever information would be conveyed during pre-abortion counseling, it is not surprising that they also report the greatest stress following abortion. However, they are also likely to engage in a long period of denial after the abortion. Thus, for those seeking to heal women traumatized by abortion, it should be evident that adolescents have special needs for education and support following their abortions. They need help in dealing with the effects of the abortion, but first they need help in just "growing up" so that they can more effectively address the pain they will experience.

## NOTES

Bernstein, R. M. (1980). "The development of the self-system during adolescence." *Journal of Genetic Psychology*, 136, 231-245.

Broughton, J. (1978). "Development of concepts of self, mind, reality, and knowledge." *New Directions for Child Development*, 1, 75-100.

Campbell, N. B., K. Franco & S. Jurs (1988). "Abortion in adolescence." *Adolescence*, 23(92), 813-823.

Elkind, D. (1967). "Egocentrism in adolescence." *Child Development*, 38, 1025-1034.

Franz, W. (1987). "Adolescent decision-making and its application to sexuality behaviors." Presented at the Regional Conference of the National Council on Family Relations, Pennsylvania State University, March, 1987.

Franz, W. (1989). "Sex and the American teenager." *The World and I.* Washington, DC: The Washington Times Corporation, 470-785.

Franz, W. & D. Reardon (1992). "Differential impact of abortion on adolescents as compared to adults." *Adolescence,* 27 (105), 161-72.

Kirby, D. (1985). "Sexuality education: A more realistic view of its effects." *Journal of School Health,* 55(10), 421-24.

Piaget, J. (1954). *The Construction of Reality in the Child.* New York: Basic Books.

# 11

## Ethical and Pastoral Reflections on Post-Abortion Aftermath

*Cardinal Alfonso López Trujillo*

During a recent visit to Russia, at the invitation of the authorities of that country where the practice of voluntary abortion is extremely frequent and widespread, I heard these reflections: "Here abortion is due to the ethical void created by Marxist ideology. It has become merely a minor surgical operation." The person who made this observation did so sorrowfully. That person also informed me that, for many people, concern about abortion is principally of a hygienic nature because of infections.

However, from other information available, it is true that it could be concluded that many women were suffering from the post-abortion syndrome there. In any case, my attention was also called to the fact that many cases of repeated abortion were reported.

Speaking very generally, it could be stated that in societies where abortion is not penalized, there is a tendency to trivialize this "abominable crime." Furthermore, this is done systematically, first, as we know, by controlling language. No one wants to look at this crime in all its dramatic and tragic reality. The term "abortion" itself is prohibited. Language is subjected to a sort of "make up," and well-known expressions, such as "interruption of pregnancy," are used instead. The act is presented as an exercise of "pro-choice" freedom.

All this is set in the framework of a "mentality," an anti-life "culture." For this reason, the "unborn child," because of technical and industrial demands, is called a "product," and this "product" is seen as an aggressor against the peace and rights of those who are seeking abortion, or the child is even seen as a sort of disease. Is this not what we find in the term "anti-baby vaccine"? One of the concerns of the RU 486 pill promoters is precisely this: do everything possible to hide the cruel and inhuman action, the bloody aspect. We could say that there is an attempt to hide the blood shed by the merciless action of the aspirators after the crime, whether it is carried out "surgically" or by this new form introduced through the new techniques of what Pope John Paul II calls a form of "chemical warfare."[1]

It has been promised that, with technical progress, the day will come when women will not even be aware of their action. Therefore, the confusion that is created whereby nonpenalized or legalized abortion is licit and not immoral will have its influence on the eclipse of consciences, which are becoming, as it were, drugged or anesthetized. It is sufficient to read the type of widespread propaganda put forward in favor of abortion so as to avoid any remorse of conscience, tears or a sense of guilt. It is sin that is meant to be covered up with leaves! Will this be entirely possible? Perhaps it becomes more possible when the drama of abortion loses its force—because everything turns into a sort of social and political project. Perhaps the public "pro-choice" demonstrations also are an attempt to reduce the feeling of shame.

However, speaking in normal circumstances, I do not see how what is called the "post-abortion syndrome" could be avoided. If every sin, all criminal behavior, generates a normal guilt mechanism and recognition of the sin, how much more so then if a crime is committed against a vulnerable, innocent human being who has every right to be respected, to live and be loved with special tenderness!

I was struck in the *Nicomachean Ethics* of Aristotle by the analysis he makes of a soul without peace. He says that in the souls of those who do evil there is "civil war"! He adds that they are souls torn to pieces![2]

In the Apostolic Exhortation of Pope John Paul II, *Reconciliatio et Paenitentia,* mention is made of man "broken into pieces" when the right connections with God, man himself and nature are falsified.[3] It is entirely normal that, from the depths of one's heart, as in the Miserere Psalm, come the words, "Against you, you alone, have I sinned" (*Psalm* 50:4).

This attitude does not come from distorted or unhealthy sensitivity but from recognizing such a bad, unjust and cruel action which strikes at the heart!

This psychological development, together with a healthy process of the conscience that recognizes its responsibility, can and must lead to *conversion,* to the rebirth of a heart, but through forgiveness.

It is liberation through forgiveness requested from and granted by God, for God does not reject a penitent heart.

In this case, the "post-abortion syndrome" is overcome by reconciliation with God, the Church, society and oneself.

Another aspect which must be taken into consideration is the fact that many mothers do not have a clear idea about the implications of abortion, especially during the first weeks. Truly life-saving experiences have taken place when, through the use of the ultrasound scanner, mothers have seen their child. This is normally accompanied by a burst of tenderness which is not only instinctive: it opens up the heart to responsibility, acceptance and protection of the gift of new life.

All of this, in principle, will be more and more possible if women are not alone and abandoned. There is a great task to be carried out with mothers who are victims of real chains of irresponsibility and a lack of solidarity.

The acute sensitivity of so many mothers who repent for the abominable crime they have committed gives witness to the gravity of the crime. It is not a matter of erasing it, by hiding it or not "making one feel guilty" of the crime; it is overcoming the syndrome through conversion and forgiveness.

A particular theme which would have to be treated is the "post-abortion syndrome" in relation to the canonical penalty foreseen (cf. *Canon* 1398).

Now I would like to offer some simple reflections, having followed the work carried out at this important meeting and after having read articles published in various journals.

1. I believe we need to make a distinction between the scientific aspect and the ethical and pastoral aspect of this problem. Under the scientific aspect, public opinion is subject to a form of literature which reduces, and wants to reduce, the post-abortion syndrome to a rare phenomenon, of low proportions and therefore of no special significance. Others, however, show the negative effects at the physical, psychological and and spiritual levels as a reality which deserves to be studied more deeply and which requires special attention in various fields. Recognizing the existence of the problem, based on studies and the serious experiences of scientists, psychologists, psychiatrists, I think that it may be opportune to invite them to to carry out more studies of the symptoms in all their variety, with a more accurate precision of the effects, and with more

precise definitions of terms such as "syndrome" and "trauma," the distinct degrees of seriousness and lasting effects etc. There is need for research in a wide span of time, not only in terms of months but years, studying both short-term and long-term effects of abortion.

All this would be of greater help in providing a more objective knowledge of the problems, of the ways to act in order to "heal," in a general sense but also in a specific way to help a woman overcome the problems as may be required by her situation.

The fundamental question on which to focus is the real situation of persons who suffer the effects, the mothers who have procured abortions (and other persons involved), and not the political preoccupation which tries to show that the "pro-choice" path is secure and without difficult consequences.

2. Together with the distinction between the different aspects of this problem, this meeting has allowed us to introduce a better form of necessary and friendly collaboration between various specialist fields: between psychologists and psychiatrists, and priests who are confessors, and those who are accustomed to be spiritual directors.

We must gain a better understanding of the whole problem, while bearing in mind all that the reality of the *crime* involves, for it is a sin which, through the immense gravity of the abominable crime of abortion, must bring about a psychospiritual process, with various indications in the sensitive conscience and various degrees of depth. This sin also requires a liberation, the fruit of penance, of conversion, of reconciliation. Even if they are connected, there will be other cases of effects which go beyond this area, because of their unusual nature or abnormality, and these cases are in the domain of scientists, assisted by others. Reference has been made to the precious assistance of *teams* working in clinics, in hospitals, pro-life movements, etc.

3. The phenomenon of post-abortion trauma has two complementary aspects of great importance. The *preventive* possibility—all, especially women, have the right to know the risks, especially the severe risks, of the choice of abortion. Above all, the teenage girls must be informed. In terms of such high and striking statistics for the United States and world abortions, it would serve to avoid the repetition or routine use of abortion.

However, in the pastoral perspective, knowledge of this phenomenon must encourage a service where, without denying the order

of *truth and justice* (also in the internal forum with the various ju-
ridical implications, such as those envisaged in the Code of Canon
Law), it may guide and enlighten the wide and demanding economy
of reconciliation and healing. These are not areas and attitudes opposed and contradictory to one another; rather they are harmonious.
They can be integrated in the whole body of the communion which
is the Church, where the Lord is present as Judge and Reconciler,
the Church which has the power of the keys in the sacrament of
penance and which, when the Judge comes, will preside in the tribunal before which all must appear.

In an analogical way, as in Saint Augustine's commentary on
the Gospel incident of Jesus and the sinful woman, today there is
historically the meeting ("comprehensive" like the title of our provi-
dential meeting here) between "mercy," that is, the merciful Lord,
and the "poor woman," who is the victim also of such a grave sin
and who can and must grow and and be refreshed through those
words, "Go, and sin no more!"

4. The subject of our meeting ought to hold a privileged place
in the integral pastoral care of the Church, especially in the activities of the apostolic movements and projects and experiences such
as Project Rachel. Let this always be done with an attitude of co-re-
sponsibility, dialogue and doctrinal and pastoral communion such as
we have experienced here in these days—and we want other groups
and nations also to have the same experience. May this be how we
translate in this sad and complex reality that expression "veritatem
facientes in caritatem"—"those who do the truth in love."

NOTES

1. Cf. Pope John Paul II, Encyclical Letter *Centesimus Annus,* n. 39.
2. Cf. Aristotle, *Nichomachean Ethics,* IX, 4.
3. Cf. Pope John Paul II, Post-Synodal Apostolic Exhortation *Reconciliatio et Paenitentia,* nn. 2, 13, 14.

# 12

## Abortion in the Canon Law Context

### Elizabeth McDonough, O.P.

BACKGROUND INFORMATION ON CANONICAL PENALTIES

Contrary to what may be a common impression, the Catholic Church is not in the business of meting out penalties to its wayward or recalcitrant members. The Catholic Church is in the business of carrying on the work of salvation by announcing the Gospel of Jesus to the whole world. In this capacity, the Church necessarily functions, and is readily recognized, as a worldwide, visible, social entity with identifiable requirements for membership and established boundaries for full participation. Regarding such requirements and boundaries, in a manner similar to other social entities, the Church employs a legal system that commands what is good, forbids what is evil, permits what is indifferent and imposes sanctions in certain limited circumstances. The legal system of the Church is based on her fundamental values and beliefs and is directed towards furthering the common good of all in relation to salvation.[1]

Since Vatican Council II, the term *communio* has often been used to express that common unity of faith coupled with that human expression of faith-filled action which ultimately join all the baptized in the one great endeavor of bringing the Gospel to all peoples. It is precisely in relation to this *communio* that the Church is compelled, at times, to invoke sanctions or penalties as a consequence for significant violation of the requirements for participation or for blatant transgression of the boundaries of belonging. In such instances, the institutional Church is affirming that there are some actions which are so harmful to the common good in relation to certain fundamental beliefs and values of the whole that these cannot be judiciously ignored or appropriately permitted to correct themselves over time. However, sanctions or penalties in the Church are clearly intended as a last resort and should be employed only if other means are ineffective for restoring justice, reforming the offender, and repairing harm done to the common good (Canon 1341). Sanctions or penalties in the Church are also extremely difficult for anyone to incur in practice.[2]

The Christian faithful have a right not to be penalized except according to the norm of law (Canon 221, §3), and any law which establishes a penalty must be strictly interpreted (Canon 18). This requires that the narrowest, exact meaning of the legal text be used so that it will not be applied beyond the limited, precise instances for which it is intended. Further, no one is subject to a penalty according to the *Code of Canon Law* unless there occurs an external violation of a legal norm to which a sanction is attached and unless the violation is actually imputable to that person (Canon 1321). Imputability consists legally in a deliberate intention to violate the law, which is also known as *dolus*, or it consists in neglecting to do what is required to avoid violating the law, which is also known as *culpa*. For instances of *culpa*, however, no one is liable to a penalty unless the law specifically states that this is the case. Although imputability is presumed upon external violation of a law, this presumption is legally overturned if the matter "appears otherwise" (Canon 1321, §3). That is to say, one does not have to *prove* the contrary in order to overturn the presumption but, rather, one has to establish that something else is probable or that there is another possibility based on evidence stronger than mere assertion.[3]

In the *Code*, among the penalties which state that they are incurred automatically upon violation of the law, is Canon 1398 which establishes an excommunication for procuring an abortion. It does so precisely because, like the other offenses warranting automatic excommunication, this particular action is, in itself, fundamentally detrimental to the common good of the Christian faithful as well as harmful to the person(s) involved. The sanction of excommunication is in the legal category of a censure, which is also known as a medicinal penalty. As such, any excommunication is intended to reform the offender by limiting participation in the sacraments or in some exercise of Church ministry (Canon 1331). Censures cannot validly be incurred without a prior warning (Canon 1347, §1), and, once the offender has repented, the remission of a censure cannot be denied (Canon 1358, §2). For automatic penalties, the law itself is considered to be the required prior warning. In relation to this, lack of knowledge that a law even exists to govern a particular action is among the excusing causes for a penalty as listed in the *Code* itself. In fact, there are numerous circumstances established in law which either totally remove liability for a penalty (Canon 1322 and 1323) or mitigate the application of a penalty that is actually incurred (Canon 1324). These excusing and mitigating circumstances are quite significant in relation to the automatic excommunication for abortion and, therefore, they are listed below in abbreviated form.

Total absence of the use of reason (that is, mental incapacity) always completely removes liability for an ecclesiastical penalty (Canon 1322). So, too, do the following circumstances named in Canon 1323: (1) being less than sixteen years of age; (2) not knowing a law is being violated or being mistaken about the law or not adverting to it; (3) irresistible physical force or an unforeseen or unpreventable accident; (4) grave fear, even if relative, or necessity or grave inconvenience, provided the matter is not intrinsically evil (such as direct and deliberate killing of innocent people); (5) self-defense or defense of another used in moderation against an unjust aggressor; (6) lack of use of reason; and (7) nonblameworthy belief that the requirements of (4) or (5) are fulfilled. Canon 1324 contains the following circumstances which require mitigation of a penalty that does apply: (1) imperfect use of reason; (2) impaired use of reason, even if temporary (such as intoxication); (3) acting out of passion that does not completely impair deliberation and consent; (4) being over 16 but not yet 18 years of age; (5) grave fear, even relative, or necessity or grave inconvenience, if the matter is intrinsically evil; (6) self-defense or defense of another against an unjust aggressor but without due moderation; (7) being gravely and unjustly provoked; (8) thinking, without fault, that (4) or (5) in the previous list (in Canon 1323) is applicable; (9) being unaware, without fault, that a penalty is attached to a law; and (10) acting with grave but not full imputability.

The final section of Canon 1324 is particularly significant because it states that if *any* of the mitigating circumstances listed in that canon are fulfilled, then the offender is *not liable* to any automatic penalties. This means that, in reference to the automatic penalty for procuring abortion, there are eighteen significant morally mitigating circumstances in which any penalty simply is not able to be incurred because of the limiting requirements of the law itself. This does not mean, however, that there are no possible corrective actions for situations in which a penalty does not strictly apply. In fact, Canons 1339-1440 provide for competent ecclesiastical authorities to employ a warning (*monitio*) or a rebuke (*correptio*) or appropriate penances whenever there is serious indication of a possible canonical offence after investigation of the matter. These actions are often warranted in keeping with responsible pastoral practice and can be especially helpful to initiate informative dialogue with persons who are totally unaware of the moral principles underlying the Church's position on abortion.

## THE CANONICAL PENALTY FOR PROCURING ABORTION

With the above preliminary information as backdrop, let us now highlight the actual meaning and import of Canon 1398, which reads, "One who procures a completed abortion incurs an automatic excommunication." Analyzing this text canonically requires, first of all, an investigation of the technical meaning of the words, then an understanding of their context and, finally, interpretation in keeping with the true meaning intended by the legislator.[4]

The term "abortion" is currently understood in this canon not only as ejection of the nonviable foetus from the womb, but also as killing the foetus in any way whatsoever at any time from the moment of conception.[5] The adjective "completed" restricts application of this canon to abortions in which the foetus actually dies. If the action is taken but the foetus does not die, it is technically considered an "attempted" abortion. If the perpetrator is prevented from following through with the action due to reasons beyond his or her control, it is technically referred to as a "frustrated" abortion. Neither an attempted nor a frustrated abortion engender liability for the penalty contained in Canon 1398. The verb "to procure" means there must be direct intent and knowledge and employment of efficacious means, by either material or moral cooperation, to produce the desired effect of killing the foetus. Therefore, a natural, spontaneous abortion is not included under this norm. The efficacious means can include, for example, performing the procedure or employing the drugs or taking the physical action that aborts the foetus, as well as involvement by command or counsel or even threat, under some circumstances. Imputability is presumed upon external violation of the law (Canon 1321, §3). The penalty of automatic excommunication, as briefly described above, may or may not apply depending on the presence of any morally excusing or mitigating conditions as mentioned in Canons 1322-1324.

Having looked at the technical meaning of its terms, we note that Canon 1398 is contained in a section of norms on specific penalties entitled "Offenses Against Human Life and Freedom" which lists only two canons: one on homicide and mutilation, and the other on abortion. It should be evident, then, that the context of this canon is the Church's long-standing position on the sanctity and inviolability of human life from womb to tomb. To shed light on the meaning of the law as intended by the legislator, we can look at the discussion surrounding the formulation of this canon in the code revision process.[6] While the comments of the study commission are not extensive, they do indicate that the committee deliberately left the definition of abortion to Catholic doctrine and consciously chose to maintain an automatic penalty rather than to require application by intervention of an ecclesiastical authority, which is the case for all but seventeen penalties in the revised *Code*. Thus, abortion is included as one of those rather few instances wherein the law indicates, by means of the type of penalty employed, that the reality of the action involved places one beyond the tolerable boundaries of the common good in relation to full Church participation as a member of the Christian faithful. Nevertheless, it is still very difficult in practice for any person actually to incur the automatic excommunication for abortion.

Recall that Canon 1398 contains an automatic penalty and that penal legislation must be strictly interpreted. Recall, too, that if *any* of the morally excusing or mitigating circumstances listed in Canons 1322, 1323 or 1324, §1 apply, then there simply is *no automatic penalty* according to the law itself. Since the Christian faithful can only be liable to penalties according to law (Canon 221, §3), and since it is quite common that at least one of the circumstances listed in Canons 1323 or 1324, §1 is likely to apply to any woman who herself undergoes an abortion, then the penalty would rarely, if ever, apply directly or fully to the woman in question. The automatic penalty of excommunication for procuring a completed abortion is thus applicable solely to a person who not only deliberately and knowingly chooses to kill a viable foetus, but who also does so knowing there is an ecclesiastical norm with a penalty attached to this action and is not in any way mistaken or compelled or gravely fearful or moved by uncontrolled passion or using imperfect reason, or the like. That is to say, the full force of the negative consequences of the penalty are reserved, in practice, only for those Catholics who act with full deliberation and intentional malice in the absence of any applicable mitigating or excusing circumstances.

The same rare applicability is operative for those who may be accomplices to procuring a completed abortion. Canon 1329, §2 governs liability for accomplices in canonical offenses to which automatic penalties are attached. This canon states that accomplices do not incur the sanction indicated in an automatic penalty unless the specific violation would not have occurred without their assistance. That is to say, the cooperation of the accomplice(s), whether material or formal, must affect the particular offense *in fact*, not merely *in theory*. The law excludes any abstract or generic consideration of liability for a penalty both for the primary actor(s) and for any accomplice(s). Each instance of possible applicability of a penalty must be handled individually in accord with the norm of law considering the specific exigencies of person, time and place.

Why then, one might ask, does the Catholic Church maintain this apparently severe but apparently seldom applicable penalty of automatic excommunication for abortion? The answer lies in the previously indicated meaning of *communio* and the understanding that some actions on the part of the Christian faithful can, at times, fall outside the acceptable bounds of the fundamental beliefs and values of the Church in relation to the common good and its primary purpose of leading all people to salvation. One such action is clearly the direct, intentional killing of innocent, unborn human life. It is, therefore, the unequivocal moral abomination of abortion that catapults its parallel canonical penalty into the most serious category of legal sanction, that of automatic excommunication. Simultaneously, it is the Church's elemental spiritual compassion for the ultimate good of every human being that restricts the actual application of the serious sanction for abortion exclusively to those who are fully and consciously responsible for the specific morally unacceptable behavior. That is to say, even obviously morally unacceptable behavior does not necessarily translate easily or frequently into an immediately applicable canonical sanction. This is *not* to say, however, that nonapplicability of a canonical sanction lessens the moral evil of the action in question or that other appropriate pastoral action, such as those mentioned above provided in Canons 1339 or 1340, should not be employed.

However, even should the automatic excommunication for abortion actually be incurred, the penalty must be remitted if the offender is truly penitent and at least promises to do what is possible to repair the harm done and the scandal given (Canons 1347, §2 and 1358, §1). Further, this penalty is covered by the provisions of

Canon 1357, §§1 and 2, which permit remission in sacramental confession of any automatic excommunication that has not been officially declared as such by a competent ecclesiastical authority. The confessor can remit the penalty provided he judges that it would be difficult for the penitent to remain without absolution during the time it would take for him to approach the bishop to be granted the faculty to remit the penalty. Priests are often delegated by their bishop to remit the penalty of Canon 1398 in order to obviate the need for seeking the faculty in specific instances. In addition, it is important to note that Canon 1357 specifically directs the confessor to assign an appropriate penance which relates to reparation for the harm done and the scandal given. Thus, for example, in the case of abortion, it would behoove confessors to be aware of both its psychological import and its ongoing ramifications so that they might suggest truly efficacious means of expressing positive and constructive repentance for the action. Readers should note that the point of the canon is clear and recalls the primary motivation for employing any sanction, namely, the concern of the Church for effecting reform of the offender or restoration of justice or repair of scandal within the ecclesial *communio*. The law itself states that sanctions should never be utilized to accomplish these objectives unless positive results cannot be effected by other, nonpenal, pastoral means (Canon 1341).

To conclude where we began, then, it is hoped the above brief exposition makes clear that the Catholic Church certainly is not in the business of meting out penalties to wayward or recalcitrant members of the Christian faithful. Rather, the Church is indeed very much concerned with announcing the salvation offered by the Gospel of Jesus, known and lived in its fullness, to the whole world. In some sense, when correctly understood, the canon law context of the penalty for abortion is fundamentally pedagogical, as well as pastoral, and is actually quite consonant with this evangelizing mission of the Church.

## NOTES

1. For readers interested in a fuller explanation of the relationship between values and law, as well as the function of law in the Christian community, see Ladislas Örsy, *Theology and Canon Law* (Collegeville, MN: Liturgical Press, 1992), Chapter 4: "Values and Laws," pp. 89-102.

2. An analysis of sanctions in the revised *Code of Canon Law* can be found in Elizabeth McDonough, "A *Novus Habitus Mentis* for Sanctions in the Church," *The Jurist* 48 (1988) 727-746.

3. The notion of canonical liability is explained in Michael Hughes, "The Presumptions of Imputability in Canon 1321, §3," *Studia Canonica* 21 (1987) 19-36 and in Elizabeth McDonough, "A *Gloss* on Canon 1321," *Studia Canonica* 21 (1987) 381-390.

4. References for this technical analysis of Canon 1398 include: Alphonse Borras, *L'excommunication dans le nouveau code de droit canonique* (Paris: Desclée, 1987), especially pp. 66-70; E. Caparros, M. Thériault, J. Thorn, eds., *Code of Canon Law Annotated* (Montréal: Wilson & Lafleur Limitée, 1993); and L. De Echeverria, ed., *Código de Derecho Canónico* (Madrid: Biblioteca de Autores Christianos, 1984).

5. Under the former (1917) *Code of Canon Law*, abortion was technically understood as ejection of a live, nonviable foetus from the womb, whereas killing of the foetus in the womb was termed "feticide," and this did not technically meet the requirements for abortion as such. Because recent techniques for abortion regularly include killing the foetus prior to ejection from the womb, an authentic interpretation of Canon 1398 (that is, binding regarding its meaning) was issued on 25 November 1988 and included feticide at any time in any form as technically qualifying canonically as abortion with respect to this canon. See *Acta Apostolicae Sedis* 80 (1988) 1818; and see Lawrence G. Wrenn, *Authentic Interpretations on the 1983 Code* (Washington, DC: Canon Law Society of America, 1993), pp. 48-49.

6. *Communicationes IX* (1977) 317. This journal, issued since 1969 by the Pontifical Commission for Revision of the Code of Canon Law, presents the actual comments of the study commission members (with names deleted) in relation to the canons being discussed.

# 13

## Project Rachel: Faith in Action, A Ministry of Compassion and Caring

### Vicki Thorn

> My grief is incurable, my heart within me is faint. Listen! The
> cry of the daughter of my people, far and wide in the Land! Is the
> Lord no longer in Zion, is her King no longer in her midst? . . .
> the harvest has passed, the summer is at an end, and yet we are
> not safe! I am broken by the ruin of the daughter of my people. I
> am disconsolate; horror has seized me. Is there no balm in
> Gilead, no physician there? Why grows not new flesh over the
> wound of the daughter of my people? Oh, that my head were a
> spring of water, my eyes a fountain of tears, that I might weep
> day and night over the slain of the daughter of my people (Jere-
> miah 8:19-23, *The New American Bible*).

> Thus says the Lord: In Ramah is heard the sound of moaning, of
> bitter weeping! Rachel mourns her children, she refuses to be
> consoled because her children are no more. Thus says the Lord:
> Cease your cries of mourning, wipe the tears from your eyes. The
> sorrow you have shown shall have its reward, says the Lord, they
> shall return from the enemy's land. There is hope for your future,
> says the Lord (Jeremiah 31:15-17, *The New American Bible*).

### INTRODUCTION

Abortion wounds the soul of those involved in it. Abortion
takes not only the life of the unborn child but in its wake leaves a
trail of pain and destruction, of broken lives and broken spirits, of
damaged families and relationships unequaled by any other injustice
in contemporary society. While abortion is promoted as a safe
choice, a way to control their family with a simple medical procedure, in fact, abortion radically alters the life of the woman. She is
never again the same, and the rest of her life will be fraught with

activities that let her try to forget the abortion experience or to justify it.

The Church, which has so boldly and unequivocally defended the sanctity of unborn life and all life from conception to natural death, has an equal obligation to minister to the multitude of walking wounded left behind in this slaughter of the innocents. It is in keeping with the call of the scripture that the Church should continue to preach the healing power of our God, his mercy and tender compassion for those whose lives are broken and filled with sin. Jesus always ministered to those who came seeking forgiveness and healing. The sin of abortion has become so pervasive, so overwhelming today that it is imperative that the Church not only continue its prophetic stance in protecting unborn human life, but it must also call to healing the millions who have been drawn into the evil of abortion, willingly or under duress, knowledgeable or ignorant of the reality, extending to them God's forgiveness and healing. The brokenness caused by abortion is keeping millions of people from fully entering into their faith journey, from fully experiencing the God-life within. The Church has always been a hospital for sinners and not a hotel for saints and yet in our humanness, we forget that at times. Because of the enormity of the abortion problem (estimates vary from 36 to 50 million abortions per year worldwide), it is imperative that the Church throughout the world address this part of the brokenness.

Women have said to me that they are drawn to Church and to the sacraments, and, at the same time, they are afraid to approach, inhibited by their own shame and guilt as well as by their perception that the Church is unforgiving. The woman who has chosen an abortion believes that she has committed the unforgivable sin, the sin that God will not forgive, the sin that flies in the face of the Creator by destroying a life He created. Women have shared with me that they had desperate need to make sense of their experience in terms of their spirituality and yet were afraid to approach the confessional because they feared retribution and shame. They feared that the Church, through the priest, would affirm that they were indeed unforgivable. The strong pro-life stance of the Church heightened their fear. As God continued to call them to healing, some overcame their fear of the confessional only to encounter a priest who chastised them or excused them. They returned over and over, trying to rid themselves of the guilt they felt, on occasion to be told by an unenlightened priest that they were crazy and what they really needed was a psychiatrist. And yet they persevered, knowing in their heart of hearts that what they needed was to encounter their God and to be healed. In countries where abortion is legal, they struggled with their sense of guilt because the society offered abortion as a solution to a problem. Solutions do not create problems, and so they can not understand this feeling of guilt. As a result of these experiences, the majority of women who have abortions typically become unchurched until they have entered into their healing.

These women share that they have attempted to discuss their feelings about their abortions with therapists who also dismissed their feelings, assuring them that they made the "right" decision and that abortion is not a causative factor in what they are feeling. This fear and avoidance is aggravated in countries where abortion remains illegal. Women have shared with me their desperate fear of being reported to the authorities and prosecuted for their abortion.

In light of these experiences, the Church has an obligation to balance its strong prophetic stance against the evil of abortion with an equally strong proclamation of God's mercy and healing love. It is the balance between the law and the pastoral. It is to hate the sin and to love the sinner. It is my belief that if the Church enters fully into this ministry of healing the brokenhearted, that God will bless that, taking the horror of abortion and somehow reversing it for the good of his people. People whose lives have been broken and who experience God's love, mercy and forgiveness enter into the mystery of life and the mystery of God most fully. The energy of God's healing power unleashed upon a broken world has the power to transform the world through love. Those who speak the most powerfully against the evil of abortion are those who speak from experience. These people—transformed by God into a new people, a holy people—give incredible testimony to God's presence in this broken world but also effectively challenge the lie of abortion.

## HISTORY: PROPHETIC CALL OF THE U.S. BISHOPS

In 1973 the U.S. Supreme Court legalized abortion in the United States. In 1975 the U.S. Conference of Catholic Bishops issued their *Pastoral Plan for Pro-Life Activities* which became the blueprint for pro-life activities within the Church. They proposed a threefold outreach: education on the sanctity of life, involvement in the legislative process and pastoral outreach that included outreach to those experiencing crisis pregnancy, and a ministry of post-abortion reconciliation and healing. While the other parts were self-explanatory, the call for the healing ministry was truly prophetic. In it, the bishops said, "The Church is both a means and an agent of reconciliation. As a spiritual entity, the Church reconciles men and women to God. As a human community, the Church pursues the task of reconciling men and women to one another and with the entire community. Thus all of the faithful have the duty of promoting reconciliation."

> Sacramentally, the church reconciles the sinner through the Sacrament of Penance, thereby restoring the individual to full sacramental participation. The work of reconciliation is also continually accomplished in celebrating and participating in the Eucharist. Finally, the effects of the Church's reconciling efforts are found in the full support of the Christian community and the renewal of Christian life that results in prayer, the pursuit of virtue and continued sacramental participation.

> Granting that the grave sin of abortion is symptomatic of many human problems, which often remain unsolved for the individual woman, it is important that we realize that God's mercy is always available and without limit, that the Christian life can be restored and renewed through the sacraments and that union with God can be accomplished despite the problems of human existence (*Pastoral Plan for Pro-Life Activities,* 1975).

This call was reemphasized and reiterated when the bishops reissued an updated document in 1985. They said

> Christ's redeeming act, the Paschal Mystery of His death and resurrection, is the cause of human reconciliation in its twofold aspect: liberation from sin and communion with God. The whole Church has the mission of proclaiming this reconciliation. Priests have the privileged opportunity to serve others by offering the unconditional and efficacious love of Christ in the sacrament of penance and fostering conversion and healing in women and men who have been involved in the destruction of innocent human life. Clergy education should reflect this reality, especially by training seminarians and priests to understand the painful experience of women who have had abortions. Many lay people, by God's grace, also serve directly or indirectly in this process of restoration to spiritual, mental and emotional health. Effective pastoral programs of reconciliation will draw upon these God-given resources to rebuild the penitent's bond with God, with the child, with the family and with the community (*Pastoral Plan for Pro-Life Activities,* 1985).

Little was known about abortion aftermath in the United States at that time. However, in his book *Love and Responsibility*, Bishop Karol Wojtyla in 1960 wrote, "Leaving aside its moral aspect, the act of artificially terminating pregnancy is in itself highly 'traumatic,' and in every respect comparable with those experiments which are designed to produce neuroses. It is indeed an artificial interruption of the natural biological rhythm with very far-reaching consequences. There is no analogy for the enormous feeling of resentment which it leaves in the mind of the woman. She cannot forget that is has happened and cannot get rid of her grudge against the man who has brought her to it. Apart from its physical effects, artificial abortion causes an anxiety neurosis with guilt feelings at its core, and sometimes even a profound psychotic reaction. In this context we may note the significance of statements by women suffering from depression during the climacteric, who sometimes a decade or so after the event remember a terminated pregnancy with regret and feel a belated sense of guilt on this account. There is no need to add that morally termination of pregnancy is a very grave offense."

Also in 1960 Dr. Mary Calderone, a pioneer in the sex education movement, wrote in an article in the *American Journal of Public Health*, "Aside from the fact that abortion is the taking of a life, I am also mindful of what was brought out by our psychiatrists— that in almost every case, abortion, whether legal or illegal, is a traumatic experience that may have severe consequences later on."

After a decade of legal abortion, the scope and nature of post-abortion aftermath began to crystallize among American women, who, as Wojtyla and Calderone predicted, began to feel a sense of guilt and experience psychological symptoms. Some courageous women came forward on the national scene, speaking publicly of their pain and began forming like-to-like support groups—groups of aborted women ministering to other aborted women (Women Exploited, Women Exploited by Abortion, American Victims of Abortion). In addition, a friend of mine who had placed a child for adoption and had an abortion shared her personal hell with me, always saying, "I can live with the adoption. I cannot live with the abortion."

As Respect Life Director for the Archdiocese of Milwaukee, I became concerned about how I would implement the third part of the Bishops' Pastoral Plan to meet the needs of the women who were searching for help in reconciling their painful abortion experiences.

In considering this problem, I inquired of priests if they had encountered abortion in a confessional setting, and, if so, had they felt comfortable handling it and confident of the outcome. The overwhelming response was that indeed they had encountered it and that they did not feel satisfied that they knew enough to truly be of help to the woman. Therapists I consulted had occasionally encountered someone speaking of abortion as a problem needing resolution, but they too admitted feeling confused and conflicted. (They shared that in some cases abortion seemed like a viable solution to a crisis pregnancy. The realization that it may have inflicted more difficulties concerned them.) Consultation with the three dioceses that had some form of outreach in place provided additional insight.

We recognized that the name chosen would have to communicate reconciliation and hope without using the word abortion to avoid intimidation and to be pastorally sensitive to women's struggle to even admit their abortions.

The name "Rachel" was chosen because Jeremiah 31:15-17 depicts Rachel mourning her children but with the Good News of "hope for her future" as the invitation to healing.

Anchored in the Sacrament of Reconciliation, Project Rachel was designed as a holistic effort that integrates the spiritual and the psychological.

As planning progressed, it became apparent that Project Rachel would have to be Church based and include the following elements:

- Special training for priests and psychotherapists on post-abortion aftermath and the steps of healing;
- Collaboration between clergy and psychotherapists for referrals and mutual support;
- Professional rather than volunteer staff;
- A base in diocesan rather than parish offices to guarantee anonymity;
- A welcoming and hopeful message;
- An ability to enter the system through the referral source; clergy or therapists;
- Development of a model for individual care;
- Consistency in the initial contact for referral;
- Confidential list of confessors accessible to staff only.

It was clear that we had to provide the very best care we could offer as a Church.

The training acquainted the clergy and the psychotherapists with their respective roles. It provided a common understanding of post-abortion aftermath and its resolution, including an understanding of grief and guilt which follow abortion as well as an understanding of canon law on abortion. Priests are crucial to this work not only because of the sacramental dimensions, but because they are men. For the aborted woman, this may be the first gentle, compassionate man she has ever encountered. His presence in her healing journey may facilitate the resolution of the hate she has toward men as a result of the abortion.

A working relationship had to be developed between the priests and therapists so that a trust relationship could grow, allowing them to refer comfortably to their professional colleague. These two groups are not normally familiar with each other. In addition, a system of mutual support was encouraged allowing both groups the opportunity to develop relationships within the outreach that allowed them to process their own reactions to the pain they were exposed to in this process.

A professional model of care allowed us to make use of the resources of the Church in terms of priests and religious as well as the staff of Catholic Charities and other diocesan offices, such as the Respect Life Office. This established base of professionals would be open to the philosophy and theology of reconciliation. The risk of causing additional psychological harm and thereby exposing the Church to malpractice litigation precluded use of volunteers. Clergy and therapists functioning in their professional capacities do not pose this problem. Post-abortion counseling differs substantially from crisis pregnancy work, because serious psychological consequences up to and including suicide are an ever present reality in post-abortion trauma. Furthermore, those who are most likely to volunteer for post-abortion reconciliation work are themselves unhealed post-abortion women who are seeking to make restitution. They do not realize that listening to the stories of other woman may trigger their own profound reactions exposing them and the client to an uncontrollable chain reaction. (After that caution, I would like to add that I know many nonprofessional counselors and healed women within the post-abortion aftermath community who are incredibly powerful companions to those walking the journey, but that healing is the key.)

Women expressed a grave concern about anonymity, desiring to see a priest they did not know rather than the priest in their parish. The shame factor is so great that it inhibits a woman from approaching her own pastor, if she is churched. Furthermore, women prefer to deal with their pain without the risk of exposure within their congregations through gossip.

The message of Project Rachel has to be welcoming because the woman harbors the belief that she is unwelcome in this Church because of the strong pro-life teaching. This initial message opens the door for her to approach the program, however cautiously. The message also needs to be hopeful because aborted women always describe themselves as being without hope. It is the possibility of hope that brings them to inquire.

We anticipated that women would enter into Project Rachel not only through the formal referral number, but also through therapists who were seeing people and priests who encountered people in other settings.

We were very concerned that the woman seeking healing be treated in a one-on-one individual setting so that the integrity of her healing journey was respected. An injustice is done to the individual when blanket assumptions are made about the course of her journey and if she perceives herself as just a "case." She is entitled to care that is tailored to her individual situation.

The need for consistency in the referral system resulted in using an existing office and its personnel as a contact for incoming calls. The referral agent needs to know the priests, religious and therapists in order to match referrals to the needs of the caller, e.g., for an older, wiser priest or a younger, gentler priest. Knowledge of the training and charisms of the individual members of the referral network allows for satisfactory referrals. Moreover, a caller who reaches the same person develops a sense of assurance and security with the program. These calls can be rather lengthy and the referral agent needs to be free to devote as much time as the caller needs. Absolute confidentiality is as essential to this program in the first contact as it is in the reconciliation and counseling that follows.

The list of priests must be confidential for the following reasons:

- Protection from harassment;
- Prevention of abuse by abortion providers who might use this list to assuage ambivalent women;
- Permits priests to move on and off the list as their other commitments allow;

- Prevents the assumption by parish staff that everyone who comes to the priest for counseling has had an abortion.

Project Rachel began with a training session in the Archdiocese of Milwaukee, Wisconsin with the full blessing and support of Archbishop Rembert G. Weakland, O.S.B., in September, 1984. While plans were made to officially announce the project in October when specifics of the ministry were in place, in fact the Holy Spirit had other plans. The story broke in the local press and wire service immediately, in part, because the religion reporter had an aborted friend who was engaged in this very struggle. The story gained prominent play because the editors were enthusiastic about the Church seeking to forgive and reconcile those who had committed abortion. In their view the Church had set abortion as the unforgivable sin. Project Rachel thus became a teaching moment on reconciliation through the local media. It became a teaching moment across the diocese when a small group of unhappy Catholics called a press conference to denounce the Church's softening of its stance on abortion by "allowing these black sheep into the Church with the white sheep who have been following along all the while." "Why," they queried, "does the Church need a special program for a set group of sinners?" Priests across the diocese, shocked by this reaction, used the occurring reconciliation cycle of readings as homily material. Project Rachel clarifies the age-old position of the Church to denounce the sin but love the sinner.

Two off-shoots of Project Rachel have been the Healing Vision Conference and the establishment of the National Office of Post-Abortion Reconciliation and Healing. The annual international Healing Vision Conference held at Marquette University in cosponsorship with the National Office of Post-Abortion Reconciliation and Healing gathers researchers, therapists, medical professionals, clergy of various denominations, support group members and crisis pregnancy volunteers to explore issues pertaining to post-abortion aftermath and its resolution. The seventh conference recently concluded included people from six countries. In 1990 a letter was directed to the conference attendees from the Vatican. The letter said, "His Holiness wishes to offer encouragement to those who are seeking to study the consequences of abortion for individuals and for society and striving to respond compassionately to those whose lives bear the moral and psychological scars of a decision to terminate the life of an unborn child. He is confident that the conference will create a deeper understanding of this great moral wound in the heart of modern society and will help lead all people of good will to guarantee the right to life and protect the human person . . . from conception until natural death." The National Office of Post-Abortion Reconciliation and Healing was founded in 1990 as an outgrowth of Project Rachel to provide a means of referring people wounded by abortion from around the country to appropriate care nearby through a national "800" referral line and to facilitate the networking of psychotherapeutic professionals, researchers, medical professionals, clergy, like-to-like support groups and crisis pregnancy volunteers to share insights, research and data, as well as providing resource materials and information to all interested parties. In addition, the office provides primary consultation and ongoing assistance in the establishment of Project Rachel within dioceses in this country and abroad.

## WHO IS THE RACHEL WOMAN?
## WHAT IS HER SPIRITUAL PAIN?

The woman who comes to Project Rachel is usually seven to ten years past her abortion experience. When she comes, some experience in her life has caused her to break her psychological denial (called a trigger incident) and begin grieving. She has often reached the point of needing to make sense of the experience in terms of her spirituality.

Aborted women describe their spiritual woundedness in this way. The abortion is for many an experience of the first serious perceived sin. She believes that she has committed the unforgivable sin, leaving her isolated from God. Her spirit is dead and her conscience is numbed, though it is the reawakening of her conscience that brings her to recognize her need for healing. She realizes that she has victimized an innocent being and she must take responsibility for the choice and the outcome. It is a major unacknowledged death experience. There is no mourning and no funeral. She feels unwelcome in the Church, but she may attend with some regularity for her other children or she may go only occasionally. Some women describe having baptized their baby during the abortion procedure, by pouring water over their bellies or over the tissue that had been removed from their bodies. It is her sense, when she attends Church, that she is the only woman there who has had an abortion, carrying a physical mark for all to see and know what she has done. She fears God and especially fears his punishment. Quite often this is focused on childbearing issues, such as fear of miscarriage or stillbirth. Ironically the abortion experience predisposes her to these very things she most fears, and, in experiencing them, she attributes them to God's wrath and punishment. She may also carry the wounds of sexual abuse and this complicates her healing immensely. This spiritual woundedness crosses denominational lines. However, Catholic women are more convinced that they are unforgivable in the eyes of the Church.

Having spoken with hundreds of aborted women, I see they attempt to deal with the spiritual pain of perceived exile from their Church in the following ways. Many of our women have made their way into more fundamentalist churches as they begin healing. While still unhealed, they tend to blame the Catholic Church for some of their guilt. They have not completely written off the Church. They are often still strongly drawn to it, but there is a hesitancy to return home. And yet, the news of Project Rachel touches them deeply. Some of these women seem to find their way home. Other women have hung onto their Catholicism only in name, being basically unchurched. These women desperately want to come home but are afraid to approach. The third group of women have clung to the Church steadfastly. They come to Mass, but often don't receive the sacraments. One old woman, beginning her journey, shared with a *Rachel* priest that she had faithfully attended Mass every Sunday since her abortion—some forty years or more—but had not received Holy Communion, having once heard a priest say that "if you have had an abortion, you are not welcome in Church." She shared with the priest that when she heard about Project Rachel she summoned her courage: perhaps the Church had changed its mind about her and she could come home after all. "This was my last hope," she said. Other women share how they have clung to the Rosary or to the Divine Mercy devotion as a lifeline. Others tell of having repeatedly confessed this sin and never feeling forgiven.

## HOW DOES PROJECT RACHEL WORK?

Project Rachel is a holistic outreach, comprising specially trained priests and psychotherapists within the geographic confines of a diocese. The person seeking help calls a central number. After screening to determine the needs, the caller is referred to either a priest or a psychotherapeutic professional. It is our experience that most people wish to speak to a priest first. The caller must take the next step and contact the priest or counselor. These might be diocesan priests, order priests, retreat directors or foreign priests in residence as students or faculty at local universities. After the initial meeting with the priest or therapist, additional meetings are scheduled to complete the process. For the priest, this means one to six meetings. If necessary during the process, the primary caregiver may cross-refer to another professional colleague for specialized care, while assuring the person he or she will continue the spiritual journey with her. Upon completion of the process, care is given to put closure on the experience, and the participant moves on to continue her life or to receive additional support through therapy. The door is left open to return in the future should additional issues surface, needing attention.

## ISSUES OF HEALING

The person beginning the healing journey needs to feel safe, and so it is imperative that the priest or therapist spend time establishing a safe environment for undertaking the journey. They then agree to enter into the healing journey together and make appointments to meet again. Quite often, the meeting with the clergy and/or religious is enough to resolve the pain, and the person goes back to her life renewed. Recognition that the Sacrament of Reconciliation is crucial needs to be kept in mind by all who are involved. Some will begin with a therapist, but the therapist must be sensitive to the need for spiritual reconciliation and so at some point make a referral to a priest when the person is ready or, with every one in accord, a priest might be invited into sessions.

The process of healing includes the following steps:

- The woman must tell her story with all its pain and anger.
- She needs to forgive those responsible for and involved in her abortion. This is an act of the will on her part, done in concert with the grace of God, which empowers her to do this. In forgiving these others she comes to an understanding of self-forgiveness and its possibility.
- She must put closure on her relationship with the aborted child/children, which includes grieving her loss, naming her child, memorializing the dead child, establishing a new spiritual relationship with the child in light of the Communion of

Saints and often having a Mass celebrated for the child and the family.

- She must hear often of God's forgiveness and mercy so that she can be led to accept that forgiveness and celebrate it in the Sacrament of Reconciliation.
- She must come to forgive herself.
- And, finally, she must be helped to discern what activities to pursue that will allow her to have a positive impact on her world. (Her companion must help her with gentleness and respect to clearly discern what is prudent and best for her at this time. Many consider moving into the public forum to tell their story. This must only be considered when healing is complete and it is possible in light of all her other life commitments. We must provide sound counsel so she will not be victimized again. Care must be given to guide them to the most lifegiving activity at this point in their lives. It may simply be to reenter their families as whole people capable of loving fully and nurturing their marriage and other children.)

## SOME REFLECTIONS

The person making the referrals needs to be familiar with aftermath and its manifestations, have good listening skills and be able to deal with emotionally charged stories as well as be comfortable affirming the caller as she shares manifestations, for the caller doubts the validity of her experience. To know she is not alone is freeing.

It is imperative that we respect the integrity of the wounded souls seeking healing. I want to reemphasize that this is a sacramental model first and foremost and not a psychotherapeutic model. We dishonor the wounded if we ignore the individual differences in the degree of wounding, assuming we know best and ignoring what they express as their needs. They become then simply a case and not a unique human being, capable of self-determination and entitled to that opportunity. The temptation to adopt a psychotherapeutic model for this ministry is strong. Such a model assumes that everyone coming to Project Rachel needs psychotherapeutic care and that everyone needs to see a therapist first before they can undertake the spiritual dynamics of the healing journey. *This is not true!* Many people have already been in therapy over the years or have done much of their grief work on their own. An abortion experience does not automatically imply a totally dysfunctional lifestyle. There is a continuum of woundedness that manifests itself from grief work needing resolution to psychotic reactions or post-traumatic stress disorder. We need to respect the needs of those calling us. For the most part, these people know what they need. It is up to us to hear what they are saying to us. It is indeed our experience in listening to untold numbers of people, that most people who call us desire to begin with a priest. There is a strong drive to make sense of this experience in a spiritual context. Nor do I believe that it is our place to make the appointment with a specific priest for the person. I believe she must own her healing and be willing to do what is necessary to commence the process. Furthermore, we must not assume that someone is necessarily ready to begin the healing journey just because she has made an investigative call. I believe that in making the contact herself she is more involved in her own personal healing and ready to take ownership for it—an active participant versus a passive recipient.

One woman wrote of her experience in Project Rachel, "Often when it pertains to anything concerning abortion, people are afraid of allowing women to experience 'hurt.' And the truth is sacrificed to a sense of false mercy. There is more concern for the 'person,' rather than the soul. But the person is dead without the soul. There can be no true mercy without justice and no justice without the truth. I don't know why my soul fled from the truth for so long. But finally through Project Rachel it was set free and allowed to fly to its Creator."

## CRITICS

Post-abortion reconciliation has never lacked critics, both inside and outside the Church. Critics within the Church have argued that post-abortion healing ministry sanctions the sin. The critics say that we don't need a special program for a set group of sinners. Others have expressed concern about the sort of Church we will become if we have aborted parents in it. And yet, when you inquire of them individually if they would want this sort of ministry available to a member of their family who may have made this choice, the answer is inevitably, "Yes."

On the other hand, abortion advocates, such as abortion providers and Catholics for Free Choice, find Project Rachel to be a dangerous outreach. It is viewed as perhaps a ploy to get people to return to the Church. Sometimes it is proposed that this sort of program is developed to "make" people feel guilty about their abortion. In an article that appeared in 1989 in a publication called *On The Issues,* which is an information and educational service of CHOICES Women's Medical Center in New York, the author, Elanor Bader, writes after having returned from the National Right To Life Convention,

> Rachel does not exist in every diocese nationwide. . . . And while it is certainly possible that some dioceses have unpure motives—perhaps they are hoping against hope to lure lapsed Catholics back into the fold by appealing to their desire for compassion, forgiveness and pluralism—it is also clear that Project Rachel is filling a service gap for countless women and their mates. The pro-choice movement's task, then, is to be aware of all efforts, Rachel included, that take advantage of emotional fragility and tell women that they should feel guilty or bad. Discussion among pro-choice activists is urgently needed to forge a strategy to deal with Rachel. One option, of course, is to run our own counseling programs. For if the Supreme Court or the states overturn *Roe,* it will reinforce the doubts of women who ambivalently chose abortion and who, months or years later, are still not sure they made the right decision. The government's implicit statement that "we were wrong, but now we are righting ourselves" could open the floodgates of confusion, sorrow and regret. We need to be there, for if we are not, Project Rachel will be the only place to turn for counseling and assistance. Our job is also to make pastoral counselors listen to women who are not 'victims of abortion,' but molders and shapers of their own destinies. At the same time, it is essential to break the misogynist theological stranglehold that keeps women in line by controlling their sexuality and their options. Not to do this leaves an enormous number of people vulnerable to the arguments of anti-abortion forces.

It is clear, however, that abortion supporters are beginning to acknowledge the possibility of some sort of aftermath, and they are calling within their own ranks for some kind of counseling outreach to diffuse Project Rachel. It is difficult for them to acknowledge the aftermath because they continue to want to believe that abortion makes women "molders and shapers of their own destiny." How intriguing that the criticism is also a confirmation of the need for such an outreach. We need to remember that within the United States many of the vocal, visible abortion advocates are themselves aborted women.

ABORTION AND HEALING WORLDWIDE

While accurate statistics are hard to determine anywhere in the world, there are some that seem to at least underline the need for this ministry. In areas of the world, like Latin America, where abortion is illegal, it is very difficult, if not impossible, to obtain data with any degree of accuracy. For other parts of the world, we can only rely on what is reported. I assume that the figures can only be greater than those reported.

In a ranking provided by the Alan Guttmacher Institute, the following was indicated. The abortion rates listed are per 1,000 women. Numbers indicate world ranking by number of reported abortions.

| Country | Rate |
|---|---|
| 1. USSR | 181.0 |
| 2. Romania | 90.9 |
| 3. Yugoslavia | 70.5 |
| 4. Bulgaria | 61.9 |
| 5. China | 61.5 |
| 10. USA | 28.0 |
| 18. Canada | 12.0 |

To show how difficult it is to assess the incidence, an Associated Press story filed in Rome, Italy in 1989, reported that in the Soviet bloc and China abortion has reached incredibly high proportions, with one abortion for every two live births in China. The article states that many Belgians cross the border into the Netherlands where the abortion laws are more liberal. Dutch doctors performed 36,455 abortions in 1986, with 21,655 being performed on foreigners. In 1987 British doctors performed 3,673 abortions on women from Ireland. The article states that one in two pregnancies is terminated in Poland, giving it one of the highest rates in the world. In the Soviet Union, the article states the average woman has six to nine abortions during her childbearing years.

Abortion aftermath occurs crossculturally and across religious denominations and outside of them. It is apparently no respecter of country boundaries, racial differences or faith traditions. In Japan since the 1950's, special mourning rooms have been established in temples for those who are seeking to grieve and atone for their guilt over abortions. The same is true in Taiwan where "baby spirit" programs have been established in temples to help parents resolve their guilt. There are support groups for aborted women in Ireland, England, Switzerland, South Africa, Australia, New Zealand, Uruguay and Hong Kong, to name only some. Dr. Philip Ney, M.D., a psychiatrist from Canada who specializes in the aftermath of abortion, has spent the last year traveling widely in Europe and Asia doing research and providing training in this area. He is discovering how prevalent this wounding is within Europe and Asia. Indeed, what we are dealing with is the need we have to make sense of our biological parenting history, that is, to acknowledge, take ownership for and grieve the loss of each pregnancy experience, whether it ends in abortion, miscarriage, or still birth. This is a human need.

Worldwide reception of Project Rachel has been enthusiastic. In spring of 1985, at the invitation of Cardinal Konig of Vienna, Austria, Project Rachel was introduced into the Archdiocese of Wien, where it was established for the first time outside of the United States. Articles have appeared in *Die Furche* in Austria, *ALfA-Rundbrief* in West Germany and *Familia Christiana* in Italy and South America as well as in *Reality* in Ireland and the publication of the Shrine of St. Anne de Beaupres in French-speaking Canada. Interest in other countries continues to develop. Since then, initial attempts to undertake the work have begun in England and Australia, as well as in the diocese of Leon, Mexico. Letters seeking information have been received from the Philippines, Poland, Russia, Japan, Peru, Uruguay, New Zealand, Canada, Czechoslovakia, Germany, France and Lithuania, to name some.

It is my belief that there is a need for Project Rachel in all corners of the world. The model is simple and can be adapted to any culture where the Catholic Church is present. Just as the Church has been instrumental in fighting the spread of abortion, I believe it must now be instrumental in facilitating the restoration of millions of broken lives. In countries where abortion is illegal, women have either sought abortions illegally or have gone to another country to procure the procedure. Having talked with psychotherapeutic professionals and priests from these countries, I believe that women may not enter into the long period of denial that we see in countries where abortion is legal. Instead, they very quickly come to realize the destruction that occurred and spend many more years in profound pain with a keen awareness of their sinfulness, not knowing where to turn for help. Afraid of their God and their Church and dreading the possibility of prosecution from their government, they suffer in silence, alienated from the very source of healing. Is it possible that one of the factors contributing to the falling off of Church attendance worldwide is the enormous incidence of abortion? That would certainly be indicated by what we have seen in this country.

## FURTHER REFLECTIONS

Project Rachel is meeting a very important need within the Church and the world today. It provides a clear statement of the Good News of the Gospel—the message of hope, healing and forgiveness. It balances the strong, prophetic teaching on the wrongness of abortion with an equally strong proclamation on the Church's care and concern for all involved. It invites back the broken and gives them the means to reconcile their sin and brokenness within a caring and knowledgeable context. It adds even more credibility to the teaching on the evil of abortion by saying that not only is abortion not good for unborn children, but it is not good for mothers, fathers, grandparents, siblings, friends and the world at large because it is leaving this enormous wake of brokenness.

Project Rachel provides a way for priests to deal with the abortion issue pastorally and prophetically. Many priests are afraid to touch this issue because they are pastorally aware of the brokenness in their congregations and are afraid to hurt or condemn people. This ministry strengthens the pro-life resolve of priests, gives them a context to homilize about it and provides them with the credibility of speaking from their experience of having journeyed with broken people at a time when the pro-abortion society screams out to them that they know nothing since they are celibate men.

The priest who becomes involved in Project Rachel also benefits personally. Many priests around the country share with me that this experience is for them a moment of conversion, of seeing that God is alive and well. Indeed, God continues to heal his people in our day and through the sacraments. They come to a greater appreciation of the sacraments, especially reconciliation, and of their role in those settings. Furthermore, they share that the skills they learn serve them well in other pastoral counseling settings. One priest shared how excited he was to be invited by his bishop to be part of Project Rachel: a lifelong administrator in the Church, he observed that this was the "first truly priestly thing he'd ever been asked to do."

I believe that ministries such as Project Rachel are significant forces in converting the "great grey middle who is personally opposed" to a more involved stance. We assume that these are naive folks who simply have not heard the truth about abortion and fetal development. I propose that that is exactly the wrong assumption to make. Indeed, I believe many of these people know someone who has had an abortion, quite often a loved one. Because the cognitive dissonance is too great, they can not admit that abortion is murder, because to do so implicates their loved one. So instead they assume the "personally opposed" stand which allows them to hold the *value* but keeps them from having to do anything about it. When these people hear the truth of abortion aftermath, they quickly identify the brokenness in their loved one, owning that abortion was not good for that person. As soon as they recognize that, they are beyond the neutral position and able to be motivated to action.

The women and men who come to Project Rachel seeking forgiveness and healing speak eloquently from their hearts of what God has done for them. One woman wrote to a *Rachel* priest "But my life, how it has changed! Never has a day brought forth as many smiles as today . . . as many moments of pure happiness and, yes, finally peace of mind. I am a different person. And I like this new me very much. I also like you Father . . . very much! Praise the Lord, you are such a patient and caring listener. God bless you for bringing me back to Jesus Christ and Our Father and my son, Michael. Today my prayers included you. You'll be there tomorrow too, along with another day full of new smiles and love. 'No Longer, then do we judge anyone by human standards. Even if at one time we judged Christ according to human standards, we no longer do so. When anyone is joined to Christ, he is a new being; the old is gone, the new is come' (2 Corinthians 5:16-17)."

In an article published in *The Tidings,* the archdiocesan paper of Los Angeles, Cardinal Mahoney graciously shared a letter sent him by a man who had been through Project Rachel. He said of his counselor, "She, in such a loving way, helped me shed all the denial, anger, lies, stubbornness and tears that were in my heart. To tell you I sinned is one thing—but I grieved my God and I was so sure He had turned his back on me! How wrong I was! Through this counseling, all the walls came down and in their places stood compassion, forgiveness, grace, faith and love. My counselor has truly been a disciple of the Lord, if not an angel in disguise! I thank God for her! During this counseling and because of it, I have made a renewed vow to my Lord and Savior as well as to our holy Catholic Church. Thank you, Cardinal Mahoney, for blessing this ministry called Project Rachel, for it has surely blessed me and changed my life!"

Project Rachel is a powerful evangelizer. The people who are ministered to through Project Rachel encounter their God in a way many of us are never privileged to do. Because they believed they had committed the unforgivable sin, their encounter with God's love and mercy is monumental. These people undergo a conversion experience unlike anything I have encountered. These people come to a profound understanding of the Church's teaching on sexuality. These are the people who now teach natural family planning, who speak to teens about chastity, who house unwed mothers and parent foster children, who staff crisis pregnancy centers and minister to other people broken by abortion. They have a profound sense of the power of the sacraments and avail themselves of them often. They are free to enter their marriages and to parent their children, often bringing reconciliation to their extended families as well. It is in being free from the sin of abortion that they are free to enter into the world and to make a significant impact on it. They are the key to healing the society at large, for when God touches them, everything changes. They see the evil of the society and set out to make a difference. These healed people are the key to ending abortion in the world. It is the truth that shall set us free, and it is these people who know the truth of abortion. Let us promote the formation of Project Rachel where ever in the world that abortion has left broken people so that God can take the evil of abortion and make from it a "new creation."

It is my belief that if we could facilitate the healing of our Catholic women and men here in the United States (the statistic used but not documented is that 30% of aborted woman are Catholic), those ten million women, their spouses and families would be a powerful and influential force in changing our society, our world and our Church.

> The punishment already inflicted by the majority on such a one is enough; you should now relent and support her so that she may not be crushed by too great a weight of sorrow. I therefore beg you to reaffirm your love for her (2 Corinthians 2:6-9).

# 14

## Personal Stories

---

MARYKAY

When it comes to looking back on my childhood, I most often find myself struggling to remember the so-called "happy stories." Today, at best, I remember only slight parts of fond moments and feelings. I have named these partial connections "my gift," for regardless of their size, they hold me and become my proof that even then, I was loveable and worthy to be loved.

My childhood was a difficult one. I was one of seven children trying to grow up in an extremely dysfunctional setting. My father was a very prominent figure within his career and social settings. He was also an alcoholic. My memories of him are mostly of sleeping, interrupted on occasion by the memory of my crying as I stared out the window so many late nights, wondering if he was all right or if he was coming home.

My mother was severely crippled by mental illness. My memories of her are countless but few of them are warm. She wasn't capable of caring for us well. In fact, we cared for her. The seven of us raised each other, and, for years, sugar sandwiches were often the menu for breakfast, lunch and dinner. There was little discipline, although a great deal was needed. We fended for ourselves. It was the clearest definition of "survival of the fittest." Rarely was I the fittest, as I found myself being dragged down the hall by my hair or hung over the banister by my ankles. My brother used to make me say awful things about myself before he would release me. With time, I believed every one.

A little further back into the family line lurked still some more dysfunction. On almost a weekly basis, I found myself on the lap of my grandfather, who then would sexually abuse me. My earliest memory of this is at about four or five years. It went on until I was about nine.

Most of my preteen years were spent fearing everything and everyone. Most of all, I feared being left, and so, I pleased. I was the one who always made things better. I was a great caregiver. I realize now, it was only to keep things the same. I could not see them as ever getting better, and so I thought I could keep them from getting worse. Time changed my caregiving stage and brought me, all too soon, into the realm of independence. My independence was defiance. I lied. I cheated. I stole. I smoked and drank and played hooky.

By the age of 13, I had lost my virginity. I was quite sexually permissive, believing very wrongly that my worth to men lay in pleasing them physically. I was taught and believed that if I could make them happy sexually, they would stay forever. It was in counseling some 15 years later that I discovered that the beginning of this particular journey began only one month after my father had left us.

One with the loss of my self-respect was what ended up being a fifteen year courtship with alcohol and drugs. There were days when I did not even know my name. With every day, I didn't love myself less, I hated myself more. They were right. I was ugly. I was bad. I was worthless.

At 18, I encountered a man who was different from the rest. He showed and offered respect to me. It was awkward. I didn't know what to do with it. I made my usual sexual advances, but he seemed so much less interested than the others. It seemed he was attracted to a deeper part of me, one that I wasn't even aware of. He was the first man who did not respond immediately to my sexual permissiveness. We dated for a while, and, though he did not respond immediately to my advances, eventually, he did. By this man, four months later, I became pregnant. I was afraid he would leave me and so, I didn't tell him. Within 36 hours of finding out I was "with child," I was "with out." There was no questioning at that time. Only fear. Tremendous fear. My only thoughts were of what people's reactions would be—the father's, my family's, my mother's. (She was already damning my sister to hell for this very thing. My child would have been the same age as my nephew.) I stole the money I would need for the abortion and hitchhiked to the clinic. I only vaguely remember the actual experience. What is clearest is making my way home, curling up in a fetal position in my bed, and rolling and crying for hours which turned into days. At that time my tears were born of fear and of pain. Ten years later, they were of guilt and of shame. But it took ten years. In the mean time, I stuffed it, rather well. I told no one.

It was on a retreat ten years after that abortion that I was re-awakened to the event. I had done such an incredible job denying my poor choice that I had actually "forgotten" this experience far more than I remembered it. It was within the experience of an intense prayer which focused on the healing of memories that all of my memories of the abortion came back vivid and strong, this time, accompanied by a great and painful understanding of what I had done. I was in the process of taking my first baby steps back into the arms of Christ, learning who He was and how to love Him. This awareness of my sin, of how I must have hurt Him, made me sick (literally) with sorrow. As little as I understood of Him and my own spirituality, I did know that He was calling me to look at this part of my life, to understand it, to mourn it, to heal it.

I first sought help through a priest who was affiliated with Project Rachel. Previously and over a long period of time, he had been working with me through the many phases of dysfunction I had endured and carried with me. I trusted him and I liked him. Liking him and wanting that in return made it difficult to reveal this part of myself to him. I prayed. I prayed constantly to care more for God than myself. I wanted to not care what he thought of me, what anyone did for that matter. I wanted to love God "for real" and to be real, myself. I prayed to be given the strength to stand alone him to confess my sin. We met for almost two hours. I began at the beginning and he listened. I cried and he didn't move to stop me. I didn't know it then, but every tear was needed. He hugged me without judgment until I no longer felt his arms but the arms of Jesus. I felt only the warmth of Christ, his love and his true forgiveness.

There was also something more, though I didn't understand it then. I felt needed. This wonder-filled sacrament came to fullness with the baptism of my child. I was certain that my child was a boy and that he was in heaven. I named him Benjamin and placed him in the arms of the Virgin Mary. He's with her now. I believe that. Before I left for home that day, this priest looked at me and said, "I love you. Thank you for giving yourself to Jesus." As he saw me to the door, he spoke once more: "This is the day the Lord has made." I smiled because I knew it. How good it was to know.

My life has been so tremendously blessed. In my desiring wholeness, God has always placed me in such loving, caring arms. There's so much to move through: fear, anger, resentment, denial, shame, guilt. I was brought to an overwhelming degree of healing through the efforts of this priest and Vicki Thorn, the founder and president of Project Rachel. Vicki has helped me to discover beautiful places within myself that I never knew existed. She has challenged me to search longer and harder than I ever cared to search, and I discover more. She has helped me to overcome the pain that comes from doing what I've done without ever erasing its evil reality. Most important to me is the "spiritual sense" she helps me to make of the events of my life—the mistakes, the joy, the hurt, the growth—it's all a part of a plan. I don't know how one gets through this without believing in God, without knowing that Jesus and Mary walks with her/him.

In my healing journey of more than four years, I have come to believe that for wanting to be whole, it is so. To be healed, my wanting is essential. In response to my yearning, my Lord is very strong within me, causing me to work hard at becoming who He created me to be, regardless of the cost, which is pain of every sort and depth. He has taught me how to unite my pain with his, and my suffering seems small. He has drawn me over and over again to be comforted in his Sacrament of Reconciliation. He feeds and gives me nourishment with his own self in the Eucharist. I look forward to receiving Him as I ask his acceptance of me as his own. I believe that indeed he dwells in me, healing and blessing the still broken places, making stronger those He has healed. He lives in me and causes me to hear vividly what I could barely make out, let alone understand some four years before: "I need you." I hear this every day now, many different times.

Finally, I understand and am moved by my deep love for Him to respond. I am in awe of how far He's brought me, of how far we have traveled together. Our travels have made us harmonious. He "eats with sinners" and I understand just how He can, just why He does. I look to Him and listen keenly now. He speaks: "I have taught you so that you may teach. I have healed you so that you many heal. I bring you new life so that you can bring new life. Please help me."

He is lovely and precious and alive in me, and I—I am lovely and precious and alive in Him. Often, early in the morning when I am alone with Jesus and my Mother in prayer, I ask for the gift of being them to others. My mind then becomes flooded with the souls they have placed within my care—souls with worries and concerns, sin and shame, sorrow. They have placed so many within my arms, only to bless me further with my witness of their healing and the birth of their self-acceptance and new found worthiness to be loved. My mind becomes flooded with the souls I have held, and at once I recognize that I have been given the gift of being who so many have been for me:. "Christ."

His kingdom comes on earth, as it is in heaven.


LIANE

I am a pro-life Catholic woman, raised in a pro-life Catholic family. I went to Catholic schools, worked in a Catholic convent, attended Mass at least once a week—and I was able to allow myself to have two abortions.

I grew up in an alcoholic family—third oldest of eight children. I had a lot of responsibilities put on me at a young age, with a feeling of being robbed of my childhood. I had been sexually abused for two years by a family friend when I was nine and ten years old, lost my virginity by a rape in high school, and had an overall poor self-image. I did not feel I was a good person, much less a person that someone would love. I felt like I was a nobody.

When I was 19, I went out on my own to be away from the responsibilities put on me as being one of the oldest in a family. I was enjoying working to support myself, attending Mass, praying my rosary. Then I met Jim. Jim was a wonderful person who helped me to start seeing the good in me. He gave me a purpose. Jim was also the first man I was romantically involved with. We had a lot of fun together going places, dancing, seeing shows, or just sitting around talking. When I became sexually involved with Jim, I didn't seem to have a problem with it. Why, I did not understand. Was it because he made me feel special? Because I felt that I belonged to someone? Was it because after 19 years I could finally make someone happy? Did I begin to feel like a somebody?

I found myself pregnant early in September and actually felt quite glad about it. Jim seemed to be pleased as well and talked about getting married. All was still wonderful until the trip to Colorado when we began to fall apart. We had some serious misunderstandings one night while out with some of his friends for a drink. A friend of Jim's told him that he was fond of me, and Jim thought that I was feeling the same about his friend. I did not have any feelings for this other man, but Jim never asked me. He just presumed I did. The next thing I knew Jim had me in the car and was driving to his friend's house. When we got there he started hitting me in the face, yelling "Don't you know I love you?" Then he reached over to open my door and pushed me out. He drove back to Washington state. I was left alone in the middle of Colorado, two months pregnant. What was I going to do? It took me three days to get the money to fly home and find someone to drive me the three hours to the airport.

I arrived home to find that Jim wanted to get back with me. I was scared now of the future, being pregnant and being on my own. I did not have the "permission" to tell my parents I was pregnant, so I reconciled with Jim. We did good with each other for a week or so until he started talking abortion to me. He felt this was the best for both of us. I did not agree with him. My Catholic faith told me No. My instincts were also telling me, No. I did not want the abortion, but I was not strong enough inside of myself to continue fighting Jim and the other people he had trying to convince me. I made the decision at twelve weeks pregnant to abort my first conceived child. I was never the same again.

Not only had my child died, but I died inside as well. I became more of a nobody than I had ever felt before. What was the purpose in living? I had none. From that day on, I was numb to feelings of any kind. I just functioned. I functioned on a course of self-abuse, yet I was totally unaware of what I was doing. Within weeks after the abortion, Jim and I split up two wounded people going different directions—wounding others along the way.

The change in me was so subtle that it was not until months later when I realized every time I drove down a certain road I wanted to crash into the telephone pole on the bank of the corner. Once I did realize what I was doing, I dismissed it because I did not understand it. Denial. Denial lead me to abuse myself sexually with other men. It did not bother me. I felt like that was all I was worth. This feeling did not start with the abortion. It started with the abuse at age nine, conditioning me to feel my worth. The abortion merely intensified this feeling.

Two years later I met Leo, this time forming a serious relationship. Six months later I found myself pregnant again. I did not want another abortion. Leo was upset with me, making me feel this was all my fault. "What is my family going to say? How can I disgrace my mother?" He was concerned about my being a single parent and felt an abortion was the best for all concerned. His culture also permitted abortion. In the end the pleaser in me took over, and

I, twelve weeks pregnant, walked into an abortion clinic with Leo to abort my second conceived child. My relationship with Leo changed immediately. I contradicted everything he said. The resentment towards him rose daily. My stomach ached every time he would touch me. I withdrew from him and more into myself, never dealing with either abortion. I never smiled any more. I was unable to have fun. Whatever life there was in me after the first abortion was totally zapped from me now.

The next ten years were difficult and painful, but I never knew why. There was no way to connect all of this together. How could such a seemingly simple walk create such a dysfunctional, lonely life afterwards? I could not connect the numerous occasions of wanting to commit myself to a mental hospital, or wanting to crash my car into the freeway wall, or cut myself cooking, or the feeling to put my hand in the garbage disposal. Who would have thought to connect all of this with a simple walk to an abortion clinic? I did go to confession, many, many times. Each time I would go, I felt somewhat better, but it did not last.

Due to my lack of self-esteem and dysfunctional ways, two years after the abortion I married Leo. It was not a good marriage although I conceived three children whom I have living with me now. During my difficult years, I was unable to bond with them, hug them, or tell them that I love them. I did not have the love for myself to know how to love them. The love I so desperately needed to show my children I had not yet experienced in my own life. What was still giving me the most pain was the inability to forgive myself. The Sacrament of Reconciliation was not helping to bring me peace. The priests to whom I confessed, through no fault of their own, did not know how to handle this situation of abortion. I knew God forgave me, but I still felt like dirt, like a rotten person. Why did the voices of guilt and shame keep creeping up on me until I could take no more and go to confession again? I went to a priest friend of mine, Fr. Luke, who was visiting from out of state, and he made it even harder for me. He smiled at me, talked with me and absolved me. Didn't he know that he was supposed to yell at me, scold me, call me bad names? I wanted him to do this to me because I did not like myself, but instead he became Jesus to me. This was painful, but it helped me to begin realizing I was worth something and maybe I was not dirt after all.

I was 32 years old when I began praying for a priest to help me sort all of this out, to direct me and guide me back to God and reality. God in his everloving timing made me wait awhile until He knew I was totally ready to undergo my painful death-to-resurrection journey. When Fr. Joseph and I started this journey together, I told him my whole life story excluding two details—the two abortions. During the few months that had passed, I gained great trust in Fr. Joseph but the fear of telling him and then being rejected was too much for me. I left the state for a vacation and wrote him a letter. The minutes seemed like hours as I stood at the mailbox gaining the courage to drop the letter in. Once I did, my secret would be out.

I dropped it in and grew anxious day by day, wondering what Fr. Joseph was thinking about me, how I was sure he would hate me and not want to see me any more. One thing was for sure, I was breaking out of my denial at last. When I wrote this letter, it was the first time I had cried over my children. It was an uncontrollable cry—deep sorrow.

When I arrived back in Seattle, there was a letter waiting for me from Father. This was a letter that turned my life around. He was gentle and loving towards me, telling me how brave I was to reveal all this to him, that he does not judge me and how we all make mistakes but the way forward is not to beat ourselves up but to try to understand why we do things we are ashamed of and then be gentle with ourselves. Try it!! I cried and thanked God who knew how much I needed to hear those consoling words. To be gentle with myself was a new, learning experience, and it would be painful because I had to learn to love myself. It was that warm summer day in August 1988 that I made the decision to love myself, and the healing process began.

Learning to love myself seemed rather painful, especially when a deep, suicidal depression came over me about six months into this process. I dealt with it by lying in bed at night, meditating on God's forgiveness of me. The voices of guilt and shame still screamed out at me. I combated this by continuing to believe from the depth of my soul that I was forgiven. In my journal I wrote page after page of I AM SPECIAL and GOD DOES NOT MAKE JUNK. At this time, my guardian angel became a big part of my life. I prayed my angel prayer, reminding him he was to guard me from the evil one, guide me to the truth, bring the light of Jesus to me, and make sure Jesus ruled over me. Through counseling and praying with Fr. Joseph, I was constantly reassured that I was not a rotten person and that I had been forgiven. Many times I could not tell him how I was feeling. I could only say, "Please listen to what I am not saying." With his interest in listening to me, his constant encouragement and belief in me, I began to believe in myself more and more.

My search for healing within the Catholic Church continued, but I could not find proper help from any one in the Church to deal with post-abortive women, so I joined a Protestant-based support group called Open Arms. It was with these post-abortive women that I began to learn I was not crazy. The others had experienced the same feelings and behaviors as I did. It felt good to be fully understood. When I finished up the support group, I had a new outlook on life, but was not fully forgiving myself yet.

I was continuing to work with Fr. Joseph on my self-esteem and desperately needing to connect with other Catholic women who shared similar experiences. Six months later I began attending healing retreat weekends at a Catholic retreat center in Seattle dealing with sexual abuse and adult children of alcoholics. As a result, I began to have a deeper outlook on life. My self-esteem began to rise rapidly. The fog and confusion I had for so many years was being lifted, and I was experiencing a new spring, a new resurrection. I was able to grasp the truth that I was a child of God. My spiritual life was growing deeper and deeper each day. There was still a deep hunger within me for my Catholic faith, to know I was accepted in the Church, to believe deeper in our Lord as the great healer, to believe everything He said.

At the retreat center each weekend Fr. Jac Campbell, director of Landings, a Paulist program for welcoming returning Catholics, came and celebrated Saturday evening mass with us. Afterwards, Fr. Jac and I would have in-depth discussions about my situation. It was during these weekends that I was inspired to look deeper into the Mass, to understand its meaning in power and in healing. I knew there was a meaning behind every word that was spoken at Mass. There were four specific phrases which kept inspiring me: I BELIEVE IN THE HOLY SPIRIT, THE LORD, THE GIVER OF LIFE; LAMB OF GOD, YOU TAKE AWAY THE SINS OF THE WORLD, HAVE MERCY ON US; LAMB OF GOD, YOU TAKE AWAY THE SINS OF THE WORLD, GRANT US PEACE; LORD, I AM NOT WORTHY TO RECEIVE YOU, BUT ONLY SAY THE WORD AND I SHALL BE HEALED. The power of these phrases was telling me that the Holy Spirit, the Giver of Life, does not desire me to live in death. The Lamb of God has taken away my sin. He has had mercy on me and He will grant me peace in my heart.

And even though I am not worthy to receive Him, our Lord is healing me through his gift of the sacrament. That understanding was what I needed to bring my healing to a climax. Through the Mass, I rapidly became a changed person. I became in love with life itself, finding new meaning in everything I did. I began to bond closer with my three children and have fun, the fun that I did not know existed before. I was finally learning how to live.

While I was attending these weekend retreats and being so full of life, the idea came to me of the need for a Catholic-based support group for Catholic women who have had an abortion. I wanted all the suffering post-abortive women to feel the love of God as I did so intensely. My healing process was helped by the Protestant support group, but there were major obstacles for me as a Catholic. The scriptures were used in a way that was too fundamental, and there was no connection to the Mass, the Sacrament of Reconciliation, no priest who represented the authority of the Church, and no other women to share my Catholic faith with. For me this was a very lonely feeling, one that I knew other Catholic women would also experience.

As I discussed my idea with Fr. Jac, he shared with me that many women leave the Catholic faith due to having had an abortion. They no longer feel welcomed—they feel alienated and/or rejected. From the pain that I felt for and with these women—knowing that up to 35 - 40% of abortions are performed on Catholic women, and knowing the fear that goes with it of admitting to anyone an abortion experience—a desire to do something for our Catholic women grew stronger. I began working on starting a support group when I heard about Vicki Thorn coming to Seattle for a conference in July of 1991. Fr. Joseph, myself, and four other women out of the many who attended her talk, met with Vicki at lunch to discuss how to bring Project Rachel to Seattle.

For the next seven months, with the help of our archbishop, Thomas Murphy, we organized an "Information Day," inviting all priests, counselors, lay ministers, and laity to learn more about Project Rachel. In February 1992, Vicki flew out to be our guest speaker. She related to all present the painful aftereffects of abortion and what we can do to help all concerned. At this workshop, I gave my testimony of how my brother, Jesus, had touched and healed me through his sacraments, through CHOOSING to believe in His every word even when I did not feel it. I shared the pain centered around an abortion experience and the hope for new life through healing. There is hope, a great deal of hope.

In December of 1992, we had our training workshop for the priests and counselors who had attended the Information Day and wanted to be more a part of Project Rachel. Fr. Blair Raum and Sr. Paula Vandegaer agreed to fly out and do the training. By October 1993, we were fully in place with the necessary funding, our toll-free number, trained professionals, and Project Rachel support group (Catholic-based) facilitators trained. For me, this has been a hope turned into reality. Not only are we assisting in the healing of women, but of the men and children affected by abortion as well. Families can be made whole again to spread this peace and love to others. Our actions, good or bad, have a rippling effect on others.

Each day I continue to grow stronger in my faith and with my belief in myself. Leo and I were divorced, and I have since remarried. This time I am in a holy sacramental marriage with a devout Catholic who shares his faith with us in beautiful self-sacrificing ways. I have been given the privilege of personally knowing the meaning of another sacrament. I could not have dreamed marriage would be so fulfilling. With my husband's love and support, I am conquering the fear of bonding with my children. Sometimes it is hard to hold my children or tell them I love them, but the more I do this, the easier it becomes and the more confidence I have in myself. We are currently home-schooling with the Seton program, which has given us a great sense of peace as a family and given me more opportunity to be a mother to my children. We study and pray together and most of all have fun. The greatest gift is being able to attend daily mass and also pray the rosary as a family. I ask Mother Mary daily to help me be the mother to my children that she was to Jesus. I continue to gain much healing from the Sacrament of Reconciliation. I actually enjoy going. My children are experiencing peace and growth from this sacrament as well.

Through the help of Fr. Joseph, I became aware of my gifts and talents. I have been able to use them in ways from working with Mother Teresa's sisters in an unwed mothers home, working in a parish as outreach minister, helping street people with clothes drives and food drives, and working as an assistant chaplain in a women's prison. I am very aware that I am a child of God and that He does have work for me to do. Each person is a miracle. Each person has a right to life. A soul is a terrible thing to waste, and with God's grace I will do what is in my power to help bring healing to the souls of wounded post-abortive women.

## TERESA — A HEALING JOURNAL

As the middle child of five, I grew up with numerous cats and dogs, cattle, a monkey, many, many relatives, and the Catholic Church. I knew the Church was extremely important to my Dad, as there was no good excuse to miss Mass. Going to church was a bit like attending a family reunion, with relatives in every pew. There seemed to be a lot of rules but plenty of fun afterwards, running and playing on the country church grounds while the adults visited outside. Prayer was quite routine in our household, as we prayed the same prayers everyday before meals and going to bed at night. My father and the parish priest would remind us often of the "rules," prompting us at times to celebrate the sacraments, namely confession. I never really understood the mystery behind the sacraments, but I developed a strong sense of right and wrong. Everything seemed black and white in our church. No one talked of the in-between gray matter. I tried hard to be a good girl, mostly out of fear of the God I had heard so much about.

Leaving home at 18 was quite a reality shock. The structure and rules were suddenly gone. I was ill prepared for all the attention I would now receive. There was a certain thrill in my newfound independence, as well as a rebellious excitement in going against the grain. People were quite different in college than in my safe hometown community. The Catholic church was different, too. Now the pews were filled with strangers, and church seemed cold and uninviting. I continued to attend, for I was sure it was better to go and receive nothing than to not go at all. My expectations of the Church were low.

I made my decision to become sexually active out of fear of losing the special attention and love from a man who showed me life through a totally different pair of eyes. I remember feeling afraid of the new direction my life was taking. I wondered what would happen to me, choosing to live out a sin, knowing premarital sex was wrong. I called home. My mother was gone. So I spoke to my father. "Is everything okay?" he asked. "It's strange you would call in the middle of the day." "I'm fine," I replied. "I just wondered if all of you were okay." Often we expect to receive a specific cry for help in times of distress, but all we may get is a strange phone call at an unexpected time.

For the next three years I continued the secrecy, flirting with danger, as I rationalized my decision not to use birth control—two sins would be worse. I'd be careful, and I'll end this relationship tomorrow. Congratulations. I'd finally graduated as a registered nurse, passed my state boards, and started working full-time. My future was looking quite promising with the exception of an unhealthy dependence on an angry man who was trying to control my life. Feeling more confident and secure than I ever had felt in 21 years, I ended the relationship and discovered I was pregnant.

How on earth do you tell your parents this news? I was a nurse for heaven's sake. I should have known better. I was the good girl. I would have to uncover all the lies about my past relationship. Most of all, I was afraid of having a permanent bond with the father. I went to church to discuss this with a priest. He advised me not to make a bad situation worse by adding on a marriage doomed to fail. Holding priests in very high esteem, I took to heart his suggestion of going to United Catholic Social Services for counseling. In talking with the social worker at the agency, I realized I could go away to have the baby and no one would know. I chose adoption. The father of the child became enraged at my decision, threatening all my secrets. I made a new choice. I chose abortion. After all, this was a crisis, a desperate situation. "Be strong and take immediate action," I told myself. "You don't have time to think, just act." I shared my plan with my sister. Speaking the word abortion aloud silenced us both. Three days later at eight weeks' gestation, I ended my child's life.

The deception in abortion is that you are unaware of the danger until it is too late. You desperately want to believe the physician who tells you, "Everything will be okay. It'll be over in a jiffy." It was far from over. From the minute I felt the pain, I knew something much worse was just beginning. It was as if all the good inside of me was sucked out and nothing but a shell of what used to be remained. I went home alone and tried to forget the day's events. I see now how God was caring for me even then as unexpected phone calls flooded in that night. My brother called out of the blue to tell me he was thinking of me. He had never before and has not since called me just to tell me he was thinking of me. My sister came and stayed with me. We lay in bed together, holding hands and crying. We closed the door. Keeping the secret between us, we never spoke of it for years.

The relief was short-lived as the nightmare finally seemed to be over. I remember feeling terrified whenever I walked into a Catholic church that God would strike me down for this horrible sin, knowing full well that abortion was the worst sin of all. My mother figured out the truth three months after the abortion. "I don't believe abortion is right," she said, "but perhaps it was best in this situation. I love you no matter what." She suggested going to see a priest for confession. I couldn't bear the truth, let alone tell a priest. I was sure five Hail Mary's wouldn't change anything. I took my secrets and left town, my family and friends, the Catholic Church, and God. The first year I moved eight times, lived in three states and finally took a job at the state penitentiary. I could identify with the offenders serving time for murder. I could see how it could happen. I experimented with drugs and alcohol, finding them to be my friends in dulling the pain and emptiness inside me. It was frightening how well I functioned by day, doing well professionally and always "doing fine." By night I battled with memories and was frequently awakened by nightmares of a baby crying. I awoke one night in a cold sweat with the piercing sound of a baby's cry still echoing in my ears. So real was the dream that I got out of bed and searched my tiny apartment for an infant. I did not understand why I was having the recurring nightmare.

The loss was tremendous. I lost a baby, myself, and my previous relationships with God, the Church, friends and family. In a sense, I had chosen to disconnect from the support system that held my life together. My life was a mess, filled with anger at God and myself. I was so ashamed that I continued to tell more lies, keep more secrets and deceive those around me to hide the truth within. All my anger turned to depression as I began to fantasize about suicide. I really didn't know how to ask for help or why I needed help, so I kept moving, kept my distance, and kept punishing myself.

"For He said, I will never leave you or forsake you" (Hebrews 13:5). God surrounded my life with goodness despite my efforts to self-destruct. He sent many special friends into my life that stuck to me like glue despite my efforts to shake them. Several friends talked incessantly of God and his goodness. It seemed like an advertisement that sounded too good to be true. One day a friend asked me to attend a pro-life rally. It had been nine years since the abortion. I agreed to go. During the rally, a young man started to read a

poetic letter from a fetus to the mother pleading, "Don't abort me."
I started to tremble, my heart was racing, and I felt as if I would be
sick. I ran out of the ballroom and jumped into my car wanting to
make a quick getaway. My friend was close behind me. "I'm so
sorry," she said. "I didn't realize." "Neither did I," I answered. That
night I came face to face with all this ugly guilt. What could I do
now? I wished I could turn back time, but I couldn't. I had to accept what I had done. Perhaps my mother was right, I needed to go
to confession.

I decided to go back to church. The same priest who counseled
me about the pregnancy was celebrating that day. He spoke of the
God who loves much and forgives much; that God gave His only
Son to die on the cross so that our sins would be forgiven. I didn't
quite believe that my sins were included in that forgiveness, but,
just in case, I thought I should ask. I went home, knelt down in
front of the patio glass doors, and asked, "God, please forgive me
for having an abortion. I am so sorry for what I have done. I *will
never* do it again." Sobbing racked my body, as I cried for what
seemed like forever. Then I slept, peacefully. Going back to church
was like going home. It was comfortably familiar, yet the mystery
of the sacraments still eluded me. How did I fit in? I felt I needed
to get more personally involved in the church community. On Sunday, I saw in the church bulletin that volunteers were needed in the
Emergency Pregnancy Service. I felt God was calling me, so I took
the training to become an office counselor. It was the first time I
had ever spoken of the procedure and what it had been like for me.
The memories were raw, but it felt good to talk. During one of the
office meetings, the director showed a video on life from conception
to birth. At eight weeks' gestation, I stared into the screen at this
fully formed tiny babe with a beating heart and my heart broke inside. I could barely get home that night as tears streamed down my
face. "It's over," I scolded myself. "You must get on with your
life."

I still felt like I was on the outside looking in at my church,
but I wasn't sure how to change that. I was 32, single, comfortable,
and doing well professionally. I joined the choir in church. I had a
peaceful sense that no matter what else happened in my life I'd be
okay, even if I remained single all my life. Then I met my husband.
God knew I needed him in my life. He is the greatest gift God has
ever given me, never judging my past mistakes. His love and acceptance mirrored for me the character of God. I was very curious

about his intimate relationship with God as a former Jesuit. He openly shared some of his painful journey and struggles, as well as the healing grace in his own life. It was that strong love that grew between us that gave me great courage to search deeper in my own life. We married two years later.

Soon after the wedding, I became quite anxious to be a mother. Obsession is probably a more descriptive word. I felt such emptiness each month at the onset of my period as painful memories kept flooding back of my past abortion. Why is the past coming back to haunt me now? This is supposed to be such a happy time. I wanted so much to have a baby and be the best mother I could be. I wanted to make amends with God.

I read the book "Will I Cry Tomorrow—Healing Post-Abortion Trauma" by Susan M. Stanford-Rue, Ph.D. I could hardly believe my eyes as so many of the same feelings and experiences were set in print before me. I attempted the guided imagery of Christ coming into the abortion clinic exam room to be with me. Only Christ didn't appear. I saw nothing. The newly surfaced feelings of grief were overwhelming. Why couldn't I see Christ? One day in the EPS office I picked up a flyer about Project Rachel. I called the hotline number, telling myself I needed to find out firsthand what kind of service was offered before referring any clients. Was this something that could help me? I wondered. What was the Catholic Church actually doing? I made an appointment to meet with a priest. After all, it had been 14 years since my last confession. It was time. Maybe I could volunteer for Project Rachel, since it was becoming increasingly more difficult to counsel pregnant women who didn't want to be pregnant.

I went to see the priest on a brisk February afternoon. I was scared to death about going to confession after all this time had elapsed. Once in his office, I was shocked at the depth of my emotion as I choked back the tears to explain why I had come. Volunteering was out, and confession was now referred to as celebrating the Sacrament of Reconciliation. I listened carefully as he gently described a prayerful journey to peace and reconciliation. He said it would be painfully difficult, but I could reconnect with the past and make peace with it. I did not believe the stories he told me. Nor could I imagine experiencing Christ as he suggested. But his face was honest and his voice was warm, so I decided to reach out and attempt to grasp the hope he held out to me. "If you ask," he said,

"Jesus will guide you in this walk. Share your journey with those you love and trust."

I started to journal about my experience with Jesus:

March

*I really hadn't been able to get a clear image of Jesus in my mind. Tonight was the reconciliation service at church. The service had always made me uncomfortable before because I had chosen not to participate in this sacrament long ago. Father Luke told me it was okay to wait until I was ready to celebrate reconciliation. I could simply attend the service. During the service I found myself caught up in the Spirit inside the church. While others around me were celebrating the sacrament, I closed my eyes to listen to the captive music. Just be present to God. I envisioned a little girl dancing with a faceless, peaceful presence. She was gleefully laughing and dancing, totally free and unaware of the world around her. I felt God was nudging me to take the steps toward freedom.*

April

*Reading and reflecting on the daily Scriptures during the Holy Week, I felt called to give up the pain of the past. I was drawn to the "Calvary Connection"—to bring light to my sins and accept the forgiveness of Christ in Communion. Participating in the Eucharist in church began to take on a whole new meaning.*

*I began to experience a great concern for the whereabouts of my child's soul and wondered if this child was at rest.*

*I started spending more time with God. I could now envision Jesus smiling and laughing, often reaching out to give me a strong, embracing, "squeeze the life breath out of you" kind of hug that makes you feel good all over. Christ's presence was so warm and peaceful.*

*At church one afternoon, I envisioned Christ walking in and sitting next to me in the pew. I expected Him to take his place on the altar, but instead He took up a collection basket and walked toward me. I put my desire to have a child now in the basket.*

*Today I imagined walking hand-in-hand with Christ to the abortion clinic. Many details that I have previously been unable to remember started to come back to me. Once we got inside the clinic, I started to tremble and Jesus held me very close. We sat quietly in the lobby until I began to feel more peaceful. Then we left.*

*I assisted my husband on a Teens Encounter Christ retreat weekend. At the hoot, a TEC reunion, the woman giving the peace talk led the group in a guided imagery. I imagined walking with God down the road to my heart. A large wooden door blocked the entrance, so it was difficult to get in. Once inside, I found a huge heart. My heart took up the entire space so I had to squeeze in and walk around a narrow ledge surrounding my heart. It was warm and peaceful but so very crowded. Once again I felt God's gentle nudging: take down the door and let your heart grow.*

May

*Many times in prayer I asked God for a sign of whether my baby had been a girl or a boy. I repeatedly was reminded of the Scripture, "Blessed are they who believe without seeing."*

*I went to the Jesuit garden behind the church one warm afternoon to pray. I sat quietly looking at the saintly statue holding a child in his arms. I began to weep and confessed the sins of my past, telling God why I did what I did, what happened that day, and how I felt when I took my child's life. I lost a part of myself that I could not find again. I felt intense grief for the loss of this child, as well as relief and emotional exhaustion from the expression of grief. When I walked back to the car, I knew I had conceived a girl and her name would be Rachel. Fr. Luke was right; this journey was painfully difficult, but Christ's constant presence was comforting.*

August-September

*At our Christian Life Community retreat, I was basking in the sun in prayerful meditation. I envisioned Christ walking with me back to the abortion clinic. It was the first time I could envision the clinic without trembling and feeling ill. Instead, I felt the peace of Christ and began to realize how much healing had taken place in my life. I truly believed Fr.*

*Luke now. Tears filled my eyes as I felt Jesus' comforting presence. "Suffer no more." What a tremendous feeling of relief and freedom. I strongly desired to celebrate the Sacrament of Reconciliation now.*

September 30th

*I received the Sacrament of Reconciliation after 14 years. It felt strange when I was recalling all the past sins that stemmed from the original sin of premarital sex and abortion. I had already felt forgiven, but all day I continued to hear the words, "I absolve you. . . . I absolve you. . . . I absolve you in the name of the Father and of the Son and of the Holy Spirit."*

*I continued to pray to know Rachel. I prayed for her often. I began sharing some of my experiences with my family and close friends, asking for forgiveness for any hurt I had caused them. I could forgive those involved in the abortion now. Christ's blood was enough. I still feel a strong tug in my heart during the eucharistic prayer when the priest proclaims, "Do this in memory of me."*

October

*I think of Rachel often this month. I never understood why I felt such sadness each year in October, the month I conceived, until now. It's so different now. I still feel sad, but I am comforted by the fact that she rests in Christ's arms.*

*One night I prayed directly to her as I was experiencing such grief at not yet being able to conceive another child. I felt a presence in the room that took me by surprise. I stopped praying.*

December-March

*I know I never again have to struggle with the concept of when life begins. When discussions of abortion arise and people say "Yes, but what if . . . You never know." I know.*

*I continue to pray for Rachel: to know her and for her to know me, to bond with her, and to ask for her help in conceiving again. I'm sharing where I am now and where I've been. I share my pain with her as I'm learning to come to God with my pain as well as my joy and gratitude.*

*I was given a miniature rose plant last month. I am re-
minded of Rachel, growing yet still so small and delicate in
my eyes. I will nurture and care for the rose bush, and when
spring comes I'll dig a hole and bury the roots in the ground.
New life comes from that which is planted and tenderly cared
for. I now understand why millions of people gather at their
beloved's gravesite to remember, as that ritual can bring
much healing and assist in saying goodbye.*

*I went to Jesus in prayer and once again asked for His
guidance. He took me to the garden where I saw a statue of a
mother holding her child. There was bright sunshine and flowers everywhere. I could feel a warm breeze through my hair
as I also felt her presence. I reached out to touch her face
and hair. I kissed her forehead and hugged her tightly. A
bond I had never experienced before. I miss her terribly, but
it feels good to know that I did love her, and I know she is at
peace and has forgiven me. I felt an overwhelming desire to
let go and give the control to God. I continue to pray for guidance and the grace of faith that allows me to believe in God,
the Healer.*

*I attended the annual reconciliation service in our
church able to fully participate in the celebration. God gives
us such freedom to choose our path in life. It is life itself that
is sacred.*

May 31st/Memorial Day

*I held a private memorial service and planted the rose
bush in our back yard at home. I burned pages from the journal I had kept of my journey to touch Rachel. The ashes were
sprinkled over the ground surrounding the bush. The music
"There is Good News" by Steve and Anne Chapman concluded the service with a prayer of thanksgiving. I'll see you
in heaven, precious child. Thank you, Lord Jesus.*

Fr. Luke brought Project Rachel alive for me in his ever gentle, encouraging guidance. So often I'm reminded of the words in a
song "Who will be Jesus to Him." Project Rachel was Jesus to me.

Thank you for listening to my story.

# Contributors

**Helen Alvaré**, Director of Planning and Information for Pro-Life Activities at the National Conference of Catholic Bishops (NCCB), acts as the national spokeswoman on abortion for the American Catholic bishops. As such, she is the official public voice for America's 59-million strong Catholic community on pro-life issues. Ms. Alvaré often speaks through the media, and has appeared on such programs as *The MacNeil/Lehrer Newshour*, *The Charlie Rose Show*, *Good Morning America*, *The Today Show*, *Crier and Company*, and *Sonya Live*, as well as on radio talk shows and local television networks nationwide.

She has published articles and op-eds for both the secular and Catholic press, including *USA Today* and *America*, and her opinions have been cited in *The Washington Post*, *The New York Times*, *The Wall Street Journal*, *The Washington Times*, *The Los Angeles Times*, *The Chicago Tribune* and numerous other newspapers and magazines nationwide.

She received her J.D. from Cornell University, and in 1989 she received her M.A. in Systematic Theology from the Catholic University of America.

**E. Joanne Angelo, M.D.** is currently an Assistant Clinical Professor of Psychiatry at Tufts University Medical School; she has also held teaching positions in clinical psychiatry at Cornell University Medical College and Harvard Medical School. Publications include "Communications Processes in School Consultation," *Child Psychiatry and Human Development*; "Psychiatric Sequelae of Abortion: The Many Faces of Post-Abortion Grief," *Linacre Quarterly*; and "Hospice Care: Transforming a Culture of Death into a Civilization of Love," National Conference of Bishops' Respect Life Program.

In addition to her teaching duties, Ms. Angelo is also a member of various medical societies in the New England area and is an appointee at the Good Samaratin Hospice of the Archdiocese of Boston, St. Elizabeth's Hospital.

**Wanda Franz, Ph.D.** received her doctorate in psychology from West Virginia University in 1974. She is presently Professor of Child Development and Family Studies at West Virginia University. She has served on the Advisory Committee for the National Clearinghouse for Family Planning Information (1984-1986), and as consultant to the Department of Health and Human Services, Office of Population Affairs and Office of Adolescent Pregnancy Programs (1983-1990). Dr. Franz is also the president of the National Right to Life Committee. She is a wife and mother of three children.

**Dr. Jean Garton** is an author and lecturer on issues related to the Christian Life, the Christian Family, and Life Concerns. She serves the Lutheran Church (Missouri Synod) as Consultant to the President on Life Concerns, and she chairs her church body's Commission on Women. Dr. Garton is co-founder and National President of Lutherans for Life which has 300 chapters throughout the United States. In 1985 she was chosen American Churchwoman of the Year and has been listed among the Ten Most Influential Lutherans in America.
She is author of the book *Who Broke the Baby?*, and frequently appears on the television program "Focus on the Family" with Dr. James Dobson. Her syndicated radio program "Speaking of Life" is heard daily throughout the country. She is a wife and mother of four grown children.

**James Cardinal Hickey** was ordained to the priesthood for the Diocese of Saginaw in June of 1946. In 1947, he was assigned to Rome where he earned a doctorate in Canon Law from the Pontifical Lateran University and later a doctorate in Moral Theology at the Pontifical Angelicum University. He was elevated to the College of Cardinals by His Holiness Pope John Paul II in 1988 and is currently the Archbishop of Washington.
As Archbishop of Washington, Cardinal Hickey is ex officio the Chancellor of The Catholic University of America. Cardinal Hickey has served and continues to serve as chairman of a wide variety of committees of the National Conference of Catholic Bishops.

186 \ *Post-Abortion Aftermath*

**Dr. Thomas Hilgers** is the director of the Pope Paul VI Institute for the Study of Human Reproduction, an Institute dedicated to research, education and service in the areas of human reproduction within the context of the teachings of the Catholic Church. He currently serves the Institute as a Senior Medical Consultant in Obstetrics, Gynecology and Reproductive Medicine and also as the director of the Institute's National Center for the Treatment of Reproductive Disorders. He was previously on the faculty of medicine at St. Louis University School of Medicine and Creighton University School of Medicine in their department of Obstetrics and Gynecology. He is the author of 96 books, book chapters, articles, videotapes and audiotapes. He has received four research awards.

**Sr. Elizabeth McDonough, O.P., J.C.D.,** a member of the Dominican Sisters of St. Mary of the Springs, Columbus, Ohio, serves as canonical consultant to Cardinal Hickey, tribunal judge and vice chancellor in the Archdiocese of Washington. She earned her doctorate in canon law from The Catholic University of America (1982) and lectured in canon law at the Pontifical College Josephinum in Columbus (1982-1983) before joining CUA's ecclesiastical faculty of canon law as its first woman professor (1983-1990). She is canonical counsel editor for *Review for Religious*, consults extensively for various religious congregations and has published numerous articles in canonical journals in the United States, Canada and Europe.

**Michael T. Mannion** was ordained to the Roman Catholic priesthood in 1972 at St. Peter's Basilica in Rome. His assignments span parochial ministry, youth ministry and campus ministry. He is presently University Chaplain and Director of Campus Ministry at The Catholic University of America in Washington, D.C. Fr. Mannion has authored several books including *Abortion and Healing: A Cry to Be Whole* (2nd ed., revised and expanded 1992), *Spiritual Reflections of a Pro-Life Pilgrim*, and *Psycho-Spiritual Healing AFTER Abortion*, co-authored with Douglas R. Crawford (all published by Sheed & Ward).

**Philip G. Ney** was born in Kenya and raised on the west coast of British Columbia with six other children. He attended the University of Victoria, University of British Columbia, McGill University, University of London and the University of Illinois, collecting various degrees and diplomas enroute, including M.D., and R.Psych.

Over thirty years he has taught in five university medical schools, in three of which he was co-professor and one department chairman. Currently he is a clinical professor in the Department of Family Practice, University of British Columbia. His major areas of research have been childhood autism, hyper-activity in children, child abuse and neglect, medical student teaching, medical ethics, the effects of pregnancy loss on women's health, and abortion survivors. He has written 60 scientific articles and three books. Recently he has been training counsellors for those who have been damaged by childhood mistreatment and/or pregnancy loss. He is particularly concerned with the need to provide both scientific information regarding the wide ramifications of abortion and effective treatment programs. He and Dr. Peeters have recently written training manuals and inaugurated the Institute of Pregnancy Loss and Child Abuse Research and Recovery.

**Dr. Vincent Rue** is currently Co-Director of the Institute for Pregnancy Loss, Portsmouth, New Hampshire. His wife, also a psychotherapist, Dr. Susan Stanford-Rue, serves with him as Co-Director. The Institute is an independent, nonprofit treatment, education and research center specializing in the evalutation of and the recovery from high stress pregnancy loss, particularly traumatic abortion and adoption experiences. Prior to founding the Institute, Dr. Rue was Executive Director of the Sir Thomas More Clinics and a practicing family psychotherapist in Southern California. He has conducted research in adolescent decision making and crisis pregnancies. He has presented testimony on the psychological effects of abortion to committees in both the U.S. Senate and House of Representatives. Dr. Rue has provided expert witness testimony in twelve states regarding informed consent and has been a consultant to the Office of Population Affairs, U.S. Department of Health and Human services. Dr. Rue was one of the first of clinically identify post-abortion trauma and develop diagnostic criteria for Post-Abortion Syndrome.

**Vicki Thorn** is currently the executive director and founder of the National Office of Post-Abortion Reconciliation and Healing in Milwaukee, Wisconsin and founded *Project Rachel* in 1984 while serving as the Respect Life Director for the Archdiocese of Milwaukee. She is a graduate of the University of Minnesota with a degree in Psychology. She has spoken extensively on a national and international level on the aftermath of abortion and its healing, and consulted with numerous Roman Catholic dioceses and other religious groups on the formation of Church-based post-abortion reconcilation and healing ministries. A certified spiritual director, she has also been a Birthright volunteer. She resides in Milwaukee, Wisconsin with her husband and their six children.

**Cardinal Alfonso López Trujillo** was born in Villahermosa, Columbia and was ordained a priest in 1960. He concluded his studies in Spiritual Theology at the Teresianum Insitute, and holds a degree in Philosophy from the Pontifical University of St. Thomas in Rome. He is a present member of various Catholic organizations including the Congregation for the Doctrine of the Faith, the Congregation for the Evangelization of Peoples, and the Pontifical Commission for Latin-America. His books include *Liberación Marxista y liberación cristiana* (B.A.C., 1974), *La liberación y el compromiso del cristiano ante la politica* (Bilbao - España, 1973) and *La concepción del hombre en Marx* (Ed. Revista Colombiana, 1972).